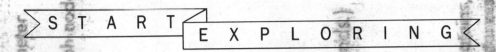

START EXPLORING

The Night Sky

Dennis Mammana

Running Press
Philadelphia, Pennsylvania

Canadian representatives: General Publishing Co., Ltd., 30
Lesmill Road, Don Mills, Ontario M3B 2T6.

International representatives: Worldwide Media Services, Inc.,
115 East Twenty-third Street, New York, New York 10010.

9 8 7 6 5 4 3 2 1

Digit on the right indicates the number of this printing.

Library of Congress Cataloging-in-Publication Data
Mammana, Dennis.
    The night sky / Dennis Mammana.
        p.   cm. — (Start exploring)
    Includes bibliographical references.
    Summary: Introduces the sky at night with stories, games,
activities, scientific explanations, and information on becoming an astronomer.
        ISBN 0–89471–764–2 : $9.95
        1. Astronomy—Juvenile literature.   [1. Astronomy.]   I. Title.
II. Series.
QB46.M26   1989   89–43032
520—dc20   CIP
                                                   AC

Editor: Chris Bittenbender
Cover design by Toby Schmidt
Interior design by Stephanie Longo
Interior illustrations on pages 9–11, 16, 19, 23, 29, 31, 38–40,
46–48, 51, 52, 61 (top), 64, 67, 70, 71, and 80 (right) by Judy
Newhouse; illustrations on pages 1, 3, 5, 7, 12, 15, 20, 30,
32–34, 36, 37, 42, 50, 55, 61 (bottom), 62, 69, 75, 80 (left), and
83–85 by E. Michael Epps

Photographs: Pages 24–27, Abrams Planetarium. Page 53, neg.
no. 322901 (Photo by Alex J. Rota), 56 right, neg. no. 37966
(Photo by Kay C. Lenskiola), courtesy the American Museum of
Natural History, Department of Library Services. Page 57, The
Bettmann Archive. Page 8, courtesy Celestron International.
Courtesy the National Science Foundation: page 78, Cornell
University; page 51, High Altitude Observatory, a division of
the National Center for Atmospheric Research; pages 65, 76
left, 79, Kitt Peak National Observatory; page 63, Kitt Peak Na-
tional Observatory/Cerro Tololo Inter-American Observatory.
Page 17 left, Helen and Richard Lines. Pages 22, 43 left and
right, 56 left, Dennis Milon. Page 6, Allen E. Morton. Pages 13,
14, 17 right, 18 left and right, 49, 58, 73, courtesy NASA. Page
76 right, courtesy NOAA/NESDIS. Page 72, Herman Eisenbeiss,
Photo Researchers, Inc. Page 59 © Mary Evans Picture Library/
Photo Researchers, Inc. Page 44, drawing by Karel Andel,
courtesy Sky Publications Corporation. Page 77, UPI/Bettmann
Newsphotos. Page 45, courtesy U.S. Geological Survey.

Front cover: Bottom; THE MAP OF THE UNIVERSE Copyright
© 1981 by Tomas J. Filsinger. Published by Celestial Arts, P.O.
Box 7327, Berkeley, CA 94707. Background photograph by
Camerique Stock Photography. Earth, Saturn, and detail from
planned space station courtesy NASA. Telescope photographs
by Will Brown. Constellations by Liz Vogdes. Back cover
photograph of the Andromeda Galaxy courtesy NASA.

Typography by COMMCOR Communications Corporation,
Philadelphia, Pennsylvania
Printed by Command Webb Offset, Inc., Secaucus, New Jersey

This book may be ordered by mail from the publisher.
Please add $2.50 for postage and handling.
But try your bookstore first!
Running Press Book Publishers
125 South Twenty-second Street
Philadelphia, Pennsylvania 19103

To Denise and Delina
—reach for the stars
in all that you do.

Contents

Introduction: Our Friends, the Stars . . 7

1 When the Sun Sets 12
2 Stars or Planets? 15
3 Which Star Is That? 20
4 Stories of the Stars 30
5 Round and Round We Go 37
6 Where's the Moon Tonight? 42
7 Shadow Games 50
8 Unexpected Visitors 55
9 How Far Can I See? 62
10 Through the Looking Glass 69
11 Becoming an Astronomer 75

Glossary 81
Further Exploring 83
Index 90

The Cosmic Detective

What Is It? 19
Starhopping 29
Let's Make Craters 48
Collecting Micrometeorites 61
Measuring the Sky 67

Our Friends, the Stars

"I have loved the stars too fondly to be fearful of the night." These are the words from a poet who lived long ago.

From his home he gazed into the sky night after night. He wrote beautiful poems about what he saw. And he quickly made friends with the stars.

The stars haven't changed much since the days of old. Those you see tonight are the same ones your grandparents, their grandparents, and even *their* grandparents

The edge of a distant spiral galaxy. The dusty material in the photograph is from our own galaxy.

saw. In fact, if you want to see the night sky that the ancient stargazers saw thousands of years ago, all you have to do is go outside and look up!

In the night sky you can see sparkling stars and constellations. The planets and the moon move from night to night. The beautiful colors of sunset and the hazy light of the Milky Way glow overhead. Every once in a while, a shooting star will flash across the sky.

Our night sky isn't *exactly* the same as it was ages ago. We have a problem that the an-

cients didn't have. Astronomers call it "light pollution." Light pollution comes from large cities where street lights shine up into the sky. If you live near a large city, you can see that your nighttime sky is bright. This makes it harder for you to see the stars.

But if you live in the country or desert, or take a camping trip to the mountains, you can see the night sky as it was ages ago. But even in the city, you can discover the beauty of the stars.

Becoming a Stargazer

Long ago, an astronomer's job meant sitting for long hours gazing through a telescope at the heavens. But today an astronomer does much more. Astronomers are cosmic detectives. They are curious about the universe around us, and they ask questions and observe the sky carefully to gather evidence about what they see. Then they try to figure out why the universe works the way it does.

To begin your work as an astronomer, you'll need to keep a logbook. This will help you to learn what's going on in the sky. And it will help you share your observations with others.

Keep notes of the dates and times when you observe, and give each observing session a number. Record the objects you observe, and if you use a telescope or binoculars. Is the moon in the sky? What's the weather like? Is anyone observing with you? Record as much information as you can.

You should also plan to draw sketches of unusual things that you see so that others might help you understand them.

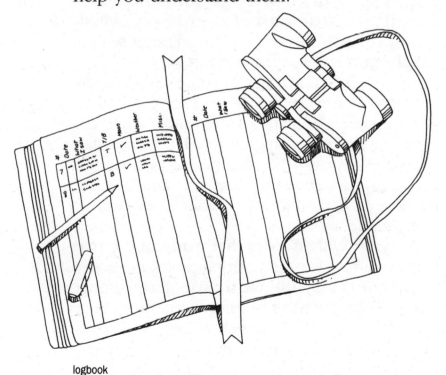

logbook

Night Vision

Our eyes are the most important tools we have for stargazing. Astronomers use several tricks to get the most from their eyes.

You use the first trick every time you go to the movies. Remember a sunny day when you went into a dark movie theater? It was really hard to see where you were going at first, wasn't it? But after a while, everything around you seemed to get brighter. It wasn't really turning brighter. Your eyes were just getting used to the dark. They were becoming "dark-adapted" (uh-DAPP-ted).

Astronomers must let their eyes become dark-adapted before they can see faint stars. It usually takes 10 or 20 minutes for this to happen. To do this you must sit in a dark room, or go outside early to get used to the dark.

Once you are dark-adapted, you shouldn't look at a bright light. How can you see what you're doing without light? That's where the second trick comes in.

Astronomers use *red* light to see what they're doing because it doesn't ruin their night vision in the way that white light does.

You can make a red light by covering a flashlight lens with red cellophane. Or you can paint the bulb of the flashlight red. Nail polish does a good job (but make sure you get permission first!).

Once you're dark-adapted and have a red flashlight, you're ready to look for faint stars in the sky. Time for trick number three. Astronomers call this "averted (uh-VUR-ted) vision."

The edges of our eyes can see faint light more easily than the centers. So when astronomers want to see a very faint object in the sky, they don't look straight at it. They look just a little to the side. This lets the edges of their eyes do the work, and they can see the object more clearly.

red flashlight

This trick works anywhere it's dark. We can use it on the night sky, in a movie theater, or even in a dark room. Try it for yourself!

Discovering the Stars

As you study the night sky, you will begin to make many discoveries about the stars.

You will discover that all stars are suns, just like the one that lights our daytime sky. Stars look like faint pinpoints in our night sky because they are so distant. Most are so far away that their light that you see has been traveling through space since long before you were born!

You will see that stars seem to twinkle. That's because their light is being bounced around by the moving air surrounding the Earth. Stars that you see low in the sky twinkle more than those over your head because their light travels through much more air.

You will find that stars shine with different colors. Some are orange and some are blue; some are white and some are yellow. Their colors tell us their temperatures. The bluish stars are the hottest—they can be as hot as 60,000 degrees Fahrenheit. Orange stars are the coolest—they are "only" about 5,000 degrees Fahrenheit.

You will discover that many of the stars have names. Some are very simple names such as *Vega* (VEE-guh). Other stars have strange names that are hard to pronounce. One of these is *Zubenelgenubi* (zoo-beh-nel-jeh-NOO-bee).

Most star names come from the ancient Arabic language and mean something interesting. *Deneb* (DEH-neb) means "tail," and we can find it in back of the constellation *Cygnus* (SIG-nus), the swan. Another star named *Betelgeuse* (BAY-tul-joos) can be found near the shoulder of *Orion* (oh-RYE-un), the great hunter. Its name means "armpit of the giant"!

Once you get to know their names, the stars will become familiar friends, and you'll expect to see them at certain times of the year. Some stars we see on warm summer nights, when the air is steady and people are out and about. Others shine only in the bitter cold of winter, when the land is frozen and the air is crisp and clear.

The more you get to know them, the more friendly the stars will become. They will share with you amazing secrets about the universe. They will keep you company on long, dark nights. And they will return faithfully to the sky to greet you, year after year after year.

You're about to begin an exciting, fun-filled journey through the night sky. All you need to do is sit back, relax, and turn the page.

CHAPTER ONE

When the Sun Sets

Everyone knows why the nighttime sky seems dark. At nighttime the sun shines on other parts of the Earth, and doesn't light up the sky. But did you ever wonder why the daytime sky is *blue?* Well, the answer is very simple.

The sky is blue for the same reason that a shirt appears blue, or a bicycle, or a crayon. The sunlight we see appears white, but it is actually made up of all the colors of the rainbow. When white sunlight hits these objects, the blue light from the sun bounces off of them the best, and we see them as blue. Since air is made of tiny molecules (MAH-leh-kyools) that do the same thing, we see our sky as blue. Without air, the sky wouldn't be blue. It would be black. You would be able to see the sun and the stars together all day long.

As the sun goes down in the west each afternoon, the sun, sky, and clouds begin to change color. They sometimes become orange, or even red.

Why do sky colors change like this? As the sun sets, its light passes through more and more air. All this extra air robs the white sunbeams of their blue color. The sky seems to turn orange and red at dusk because the dust in our air reflects these colors.

While everyone enjoys watching a beautiful sunset, they are missing something happening on the opposite side of the sky.

About a half hour after the sun disappears in the west, turn around and watch the eastern sky. If it's clear, you might be able to see a dark purple haze low in the east. Many people have seen it, but they don't know what it is.

This is the shadow of the Earth. As the sun goes down in the west, the Earth's shadow rises higher in the east. As it gets higher and higher, the sky becomes darker.

When the shadow covers us, it becomes dark. The sun is now shining on the other side of the world. When our part of Earth is in shadow it is nighttime.

As the sky darkens, the stars begin to come out. One by one they appear. Some people long ago thought this was the time when tiny fairies flew through the air and lit the stars one after another. Today we know that stars are suns just like ours. They've been shining there all day long, but we couldn't see them because the sky was so bright.

Watching for Satellites

Once it gets darker, watch the sky for satellites (SA-tuh-lites). Hundreds of them orbit the Earth hundreds of miles out in space. Many people think you can't see satellites because they are so far out in space. But they're made of metal, and they reflect sunlight well.

A satellite looks just like

This Tiros satellite was used to look for storms in the Atlantic and Pacific Oceans.

a star that is moving. If you see one, watch it carefully to make sure it doesn't have red and green blinking lights. If it does, it's an airplane, not a satellite.

Satellites can appear at any time. They drift slowly across the sky. Many of the satellites that move from west to east are American satellites. Those that move from south to north or from north to south are probably Soviet satellites.

Satellites orbit the Earth once every 90 minutes or so. They do everything from studying the weather to transmitting telephone and radio messages. Some might be telescopes that probe the universe. And others might be spy satellites.

Sometimes a satellite will appear to get brighter and dimmer, brighter and dimmer. This means that the satellite is tumbling or spinning as it orbits.

One of the brightest satellites in our sky is the Soviet MIR Space Station. Sometimes we can even see the United States Space Shuttle fly over. These might have cosmonauts or astronauts on board, but don't expect to see them. Satellites look just like dots to even the most powerful telescopes.

To find out more about the U.S. Space Shuttle, write to Publications Request and Distribution, Code XEP, NASA Headquarters, Washington, D.C. 20546.

The U.S. Skylab space station is one example of a satellite that orbited the cloud-covered Earth.

CHAPTER TWO

Stars or Planets?

Star light, star bright,
First star I see tonight.
Wish I may, wish I might,
Get this wish I wish tonight.

Have you ever said this rhyme while watching the first star come out at dusk? Believe it or not, the first "star" you see may not be a star. It may be a planet! The planets are often the brightest things in our sky—after the sun and moon. Even though they look like stars, they are very different.

Stars are glowing balls of gas just like our sun. They are very hot and shine with their own light. They look tiny and faint only because they are so far away.

But planets are more like the Earth we live on. They aren't hot enough to glow on their own, so we see them by the sunlight they reflect. They seem so bright because they are much closer than the stars.

The difference between stars and planets is something like the difference between a light bulb that's turned on and a light bulb that's turned off. The one that's on is very hot and shines on its own. The one that's turned off is cooler, so we see only the light it reflects from somewhere else.

Today we know of nine planets that circle our sun: Mercury, Venus, Earth, Mars, Jupiter, Saturn, Uranus, Neptune, and Pluto. Without a telescope we can see only five: Mercury, Venus, Mars, Jupiter, and Saturn (and, of course, the Earth!).

How can you tell which of the many lights in our night sky are stars and which are planets? Astronomers use several tricks.

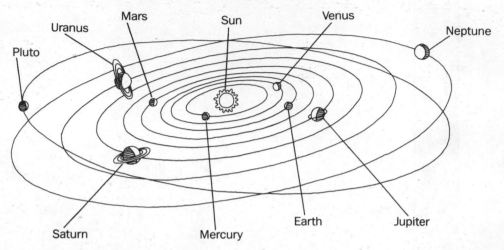

Our Solar System

Does It Twinkle?

First, look to see if the light is twinkling. If it isn't, it's probably a planet. Stars seem to twinkle, you remember, because their light is bounced around by the air that surrounds us. The light from planets is bounced around too, but because the planets look much larger to us, their light doesn't seem to bounce as much.

Another way to tell if something is a planet is by the direction it appears in the sky. If you see a bright object in the north, it is definitely not a planet. That's because the turning of our Earth makes planets rise in the east, pass across the southern sky, and set in the west. For those of us living in North America, above the Earth's equator, planets never appear in the northern sky.

The sparkling stars in this photo are part of our Milky Way galaxy. The fuzzy spots are galaxies 500 million light-years away.

Does It Move?

The very best way to tell if something is a planet (unless you have a telescope, of course!) is to watch to see if it moves from night to night. All planets orbit the sun just as our Earth does, so planets appear to move through the more distant stars.

Some planets move quickly, while others move very slowly. The closer a planet is to the sun, the faster it moves. Mercury and Venus are closest to the sun, so they can change their positions in only a day or two. Mars may seem to move in only a few days. But it might take weeks before we see Jupiter and Saturn change positions.

As they orbit the sun, planets move through the stars from west to east. This is called "direct" motion. But sometimes they appear to stop and go backwards—from east to west. This happens when the planet lies on the opposite side of our sky from the sun. Then it does everything opposite the sun: When the sun sets in the west, the planet rises in the east. And when the sun is rising in the east, the planet

The planet Saturn

is setting in the west. Astronomers call this opposite position "opposition."

Mars, Jupiter, and Saturn all can be found at opposition sometimes because they lie farther from the sun than the Earth. But they don't really stop and go backwards. They just seem to because we on Earth pass them on our own orbit. It's just like when you ride your bicycle faster than someone else—when you pass, the other cyclist seems to go backwards for a while.

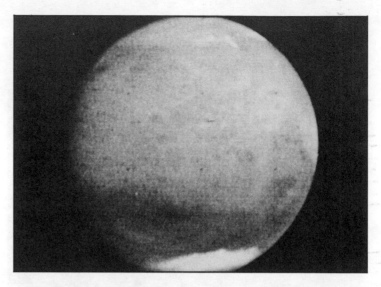

The dark features on the surface of the planet Mars are rock formations. The circle near the top of the planet is an extinct volcano the size of Arizona!

Our planet, Earth, as seen from the Apollo 17 spacecraft.

This backwards motion of the planets is called "retrograde" motion. It continues for a few weeks around the time of opposition. Then, once we pass it completely, the planet appears to go forward once again.

Next time you watch the stars come out and see a bright object that moves from night to night, but doesn't twinkle, you've probably found a planet.

So you might have to change the rhyme a little:

Planet light, planet bright,
First planet I see tonight, . . .

What Is It?

You can find out if an object you see in the sky is a star or a planet by doing a very simple experiment.

With a pencil and paper, make a careful map of the stars around the object you think might be a planet. Be sure to put all the stars in their right places—especially those close to the object.

Then, every few nights, go outdoors and find the object and the same group of stars. Draw on your star map the position of the object.

Is it always in the same place near the stars, or has it moved a little? If the object has moved, it must be a planet.

CHAPTER THREE

Which Star is That?

The sun has set, and the stars have begun to turn on their lights. To find your way around the nighttime sky, you'll need a star map like the ones shown on pages 24 to 27.

The first thing you'll notice about a sky map is that it looks very different from a map of the Earth, or a map of a country. A sky map is a scale model of the sky we see overhead. You can use it to find your way around the nighttime sky, just as you use a map of the ground to find your way on Earth.

A sky map has a circle around it that represents an imaginary line between the sky and the flat ground. This circle is called the "horizon" (hoe-RYE-zun). Because we live among houses, trees, and mountains, the only place where we can see the real horizon is from the middle of the ocean.

If you hold the map in front of you, you'll see that it has the directions north, south, east, and west written on it—just like a map of the ground. North is at the top, south is at the bottom, east is on the left, and west is on the right.

Wait a minute! Something's wrong. East and west are *backward* from regular maps. That's because this is a map of the sky. To see it correctly, hold it over your head and aim the words north and south in the right directions. Now the directions on the map match those on the ground!

To describe a direction somewhere between north and east, we combine the words to make the word "northeast." Or if you see something between south and west, it's in the southwest. You can now make four new directions: northeast, northwest, southeast, and southwest.

The next thing to notice about a sky map is that the stars are shown as black dots. The bigger the dot, the brighter the star it represents. All the dots are in the same positions as the real stars in the night sky.

Near the dots you can see words. Those written in capital letters, such as CYGNUS, are names of star groupings, and those with lower case letters, such as Deneb, are names of stars. Some words might even tell you where you can aim a telescope to see more unusual objects. "Nb" is a hazy cloud of gas called a "nebula" (NEB-yoo-lah). "Cl" shows you where to find clusters of stars. And "Glx" represents a distant galaxy just like our own Milky Way.

Right in the map's center is a little plus sign (+) that marks the point in the sky straight over your head. This point is called the "zenith" (ZEE-nith).

With so many stars in the sky, it's easy to get confused. But not on the sky map. Astronomers have connected some dots on your sky map with lines to make familiar pictures. Some of these pictures are called constellations (see page 31).

In the north you can see a picture of the Big Dipper. It looks like a giant ice-cream

The Big Dipper as seen through the northern lights of the aurora borealis (UH-rohr-uh bohr-ee-AL-is). The aurora borealis is caused by electrified gas particles from the sun hitting our atmosphere near the North Pole.

scoop with a long, bent handle. Then there's a picture of Leo, the lion. And Scorpius, the scorpion. And Orion, the hunter.

Of course, the real sky has no lines connecting the stars. But you can imagine where they might be. Just as in the game "connect-the-dots," you can connect all the dots on your sky map. That way you can see the same pictures in the sky. You can even make up your own pictures by drawing other lines between other stars.

If you watch the sky for long, you'll discover that it changes from hour to hour and from night to night. It also changes from month to month. So be careful to use the right sky map. Printed on each map is the season for which it will work.

For example, the map might say it represents the sky for autumn. That means that you can use it just after dark during the autumn months.

By holding the map up to the sky, you can see the same stars and star pictures that are in the sky, and begin to learn their names for yourself.

Now you're ready to go outdoors and use your sky map. To see it in the dark, you'll need a flashlight covered with red cellophane to protect your night vision.

Winter Sky Map

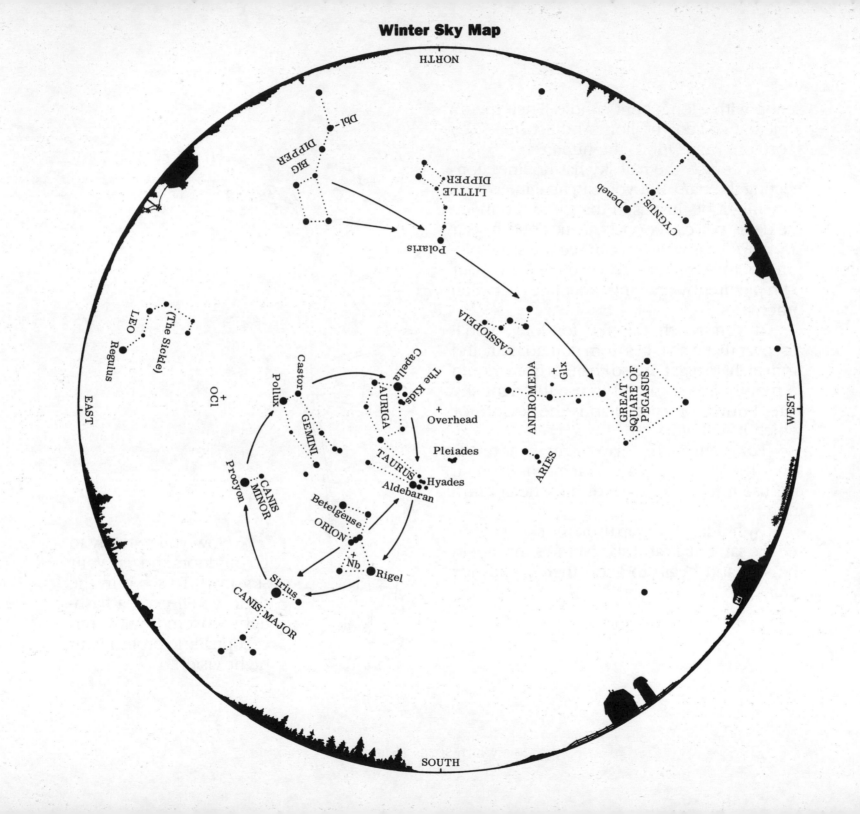

Spring Sky Map

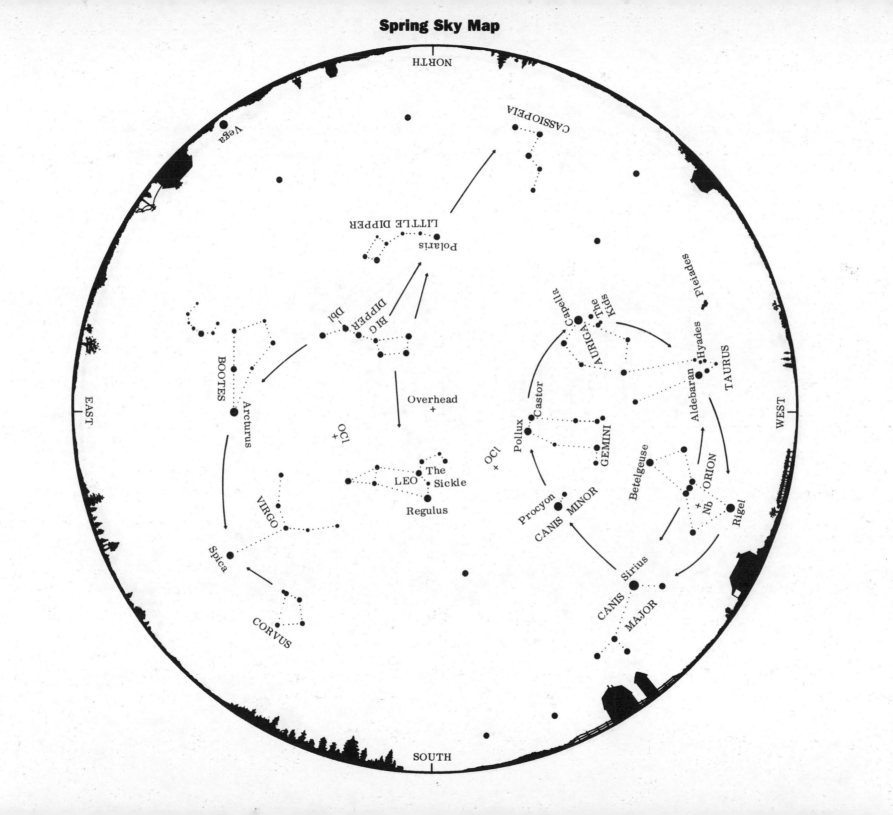

Summer Sky Map

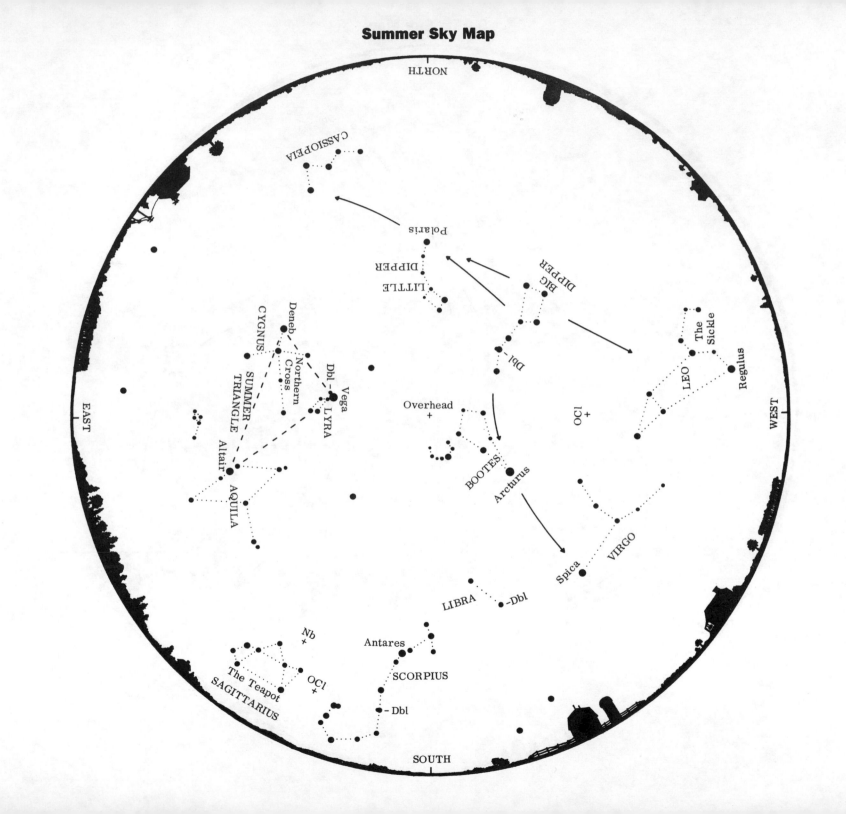

Fall Sky Map

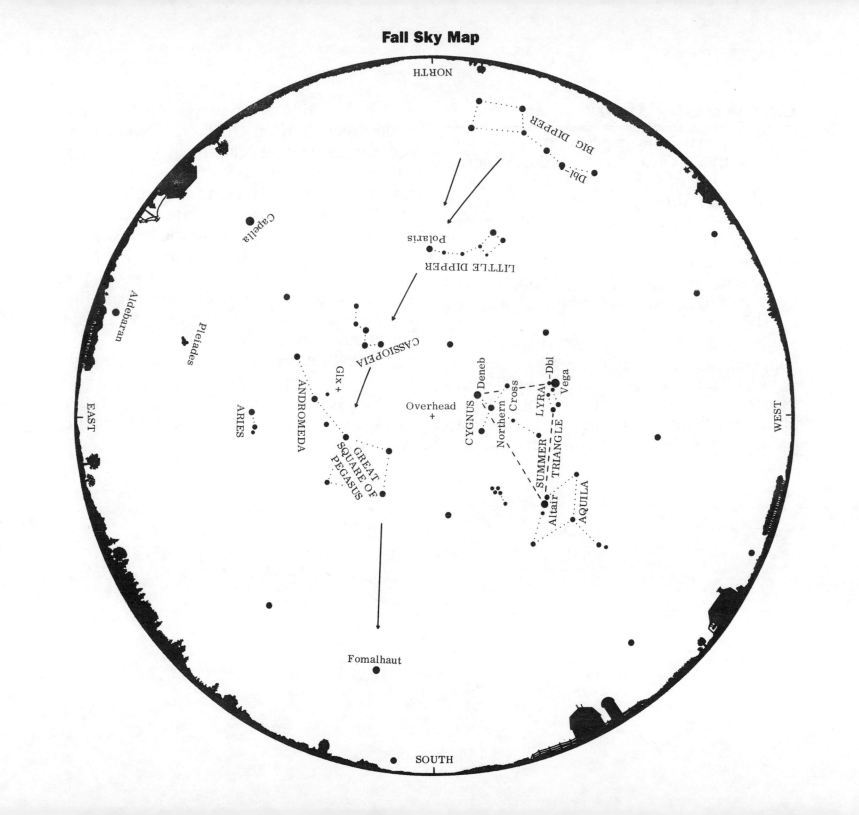

Using a Sky Map

You can use the map to identify stars and to locate them. On a winter evening, suppose you see a bright star very low in the eastern sky and you want to learn its name. Look at your winter map for a big dot near the eastern horizon. If you've got the right map, you'll discover that the star's name is *Regulus* (REG-yoo-lus) in the head of Leo, the lion. It lies in a group of stars that looks just like a backward question mark.

You also can use the sky map in reverse. Suppose you want to find the star named *Antares* (an-TAIR-eez) on a warm summer night. It's shown on the summer map, about a third of the way from the southeastern horizon to the zenith. If you go outside during that season and look a third of the way up from the southeastern horizon to the zenith, you should see Antares shining brightly.

Remember, the sky map is only a scale model of the real sky. Don't be confused: the star pictures and groupings will look smaller on the map than they do in the real sky.

If the sky is hazy or if there is bright moonlight or light from a large city, you might not be able to see some of the fainter stars. But if the sky is very dark, you may see even more stars than your map shows.

Don't be frustrated if you have a rough time at first. It takes some practice before you can find your way around the starry sky. But once you do, you won't have trouble finding anything again!

Starhopping

Some stars aren't so easy to find. A trick that astronomers use to find stars is called "starhopping."

Starhopping lets you "hop" from star to star until you find the one you want. Try this by using the stars of the Big Dipper to find the North Star.

First, find the Big Dipper in the sky. See the two stars at the end of the Dipper's bowl? They are called the "pointer" stars because they point to the North Star.

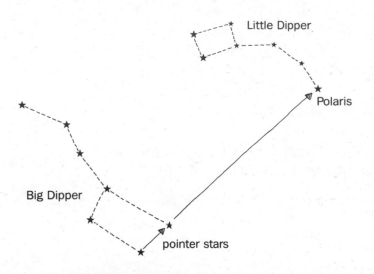

Little Dipper

Polaris

Big Dipper

pointer stars

Now, draw an imaginary line between the two pointer stars—from the bottom to the top of the bowl. On your star map, this is shown as an arrow. If you continue that line onward about five times the distance between them, you will come to another bright star. Its name is *Polaris* (poh-LAH-rus). We also call this star the North Star because it always lies in the north.

You can use other star groups to starhop around the sky. On the wintertime map, you'll notice that the three stars in the middle of the star grouping of Orion can be used as pointers. If you follow them, they point to the left toward the star *Sirius* (SEE-ree-us) and to the right toward the star *Aldebaran* (al-DEB-uh-ran).

Many groups of stars can be used for starhopping. Just look on your star map for arrows, or make up your own!

CHAPTER FOUR

Stories of the Stars

Many of the groups of stars we see on a clear, dark night got their names thousands of years ago. Back then, storytellers traveled from town to town, telling of famous people, animals, and things that happened to them on their travels—stories they told in return for food and a place to sleep.

What better "picture book" could a storyteller want than the starry night sky? As long as the sky was clear, they could always see it. And no matter how far they traveled, it was still there.

It was in this sky that the ancients imagined heroes and gods, ugly dragons, and beautiful maidens. They weaved stories about them and created images for the groups of stars we know as constellations (kahn-steh-LAY-shuns).

Not everyone saw the same pictures in the sky. Some ancient people saw the constellation of *Ursa Major* as a great bear with a very long tail. Ancient Greek legends say that the bear was causing trouble and the strong man Hercules picked it up by the tail and swung it into the sky. That's how the bear got such a long tail!

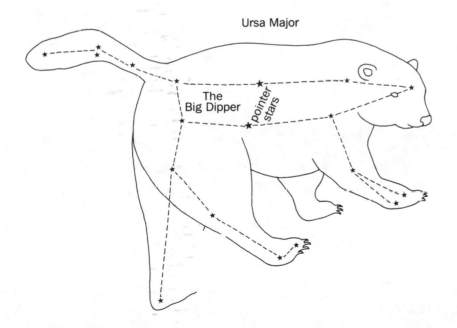

Ursa Major

The Big Dipper

pointer stars

The American Indians knew that bears don't have long tails. They saw this star grouping as a bear being chased by three hunters. People in Europe thought of it not as a bear, but as a plow. North Americans know it as a pot with a long bent handle—the Big Dipper.

The Seven Beauties

Another fascinating group of stars is a tiny cluster we see during the winter named the *Pleiades* (PLEE-uh-deez). The Greeks thought of its stars as the seven beautiful daughters of Atlas, the man who held the world on his shoulders. The North American Blackfoot Indians saw it as the sad sons of a poor Indian family.

The Polynesians knew the Pleiades as one very beautiful star that was broken apart by the gods to keep it from boasting about its beauty. But Polynesian legends say that if you listen carefully, you can hear the stars whispering to each other that they're even lovelier than before!

Some stories about stars can be pretty complicated. One tells of *Andromeda* (an-DRAH-muh-duh), the beautiful daughter of King *Cepheus* (SEE-fee-us) and his queen. The queen, *Cassiopeia* (kah-see-oh-PEE-yuh), always boasted of her daughter's beauty. This angered one of the gods, who chained the girl to a rock in the ocean to be eaten by the sea monster *Cetus* (SEE-tus). But a handsome young man named *Perseus* (PUR-see-yus) came to her rescue and saved Andromeda from death. All the characters in this story are constellations of the autumn sky.

Not all the pictures the ancients told stories about are easy to see. It takes a lot of imagination to see a ram in *Aries* (AYR-ees), or an eagle in *Aquila* (UH-kwil-uh). The two stars of *Canis Minor* (KAY-nis MY-ner) don't look much like a dog either!

Today's astronomers don't look at constellations in the same way the ancients did. Instead, they divide the sky into 88 separate areas. These areas all have different sizes and shapes, but they're still called constellations.

Modern astronomers think of constellations just like states of the United States. If we say that the city of San Diego is in the state of California, we know just where on a map to look. When we say that the star Regulus is in the constellation of Leo, astronomers know just where in the sky to look.

Draw Your Own Pictures

Since some constellations are hard to find, why not make up your own pictures? You can do this by drawing imaginary lines between the stars. Astronomers call these "asterisms" (AS-tur-i-zums).

You can make asterisms anywhere. They can fit inside a constellation, or you can make them by including stars from several constellations. The Big Dipper is not a constellation. It's actually an asterism inside the constellation of Ursa Major.

Some of the easiest asterisms you can make are squares and circles and triangles. In

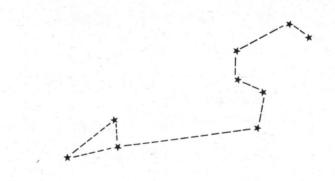

Leo, the lion

the summer sky you can find the asterism of the Summer Triangle. In autumn, you can find the Great Square of *Pegasus* (PEG-uh-sus). And in the wintertime, you can see the Great Winter Circle.

Some asterisms make unusual pictures. The head of *Leo* the lion looks like a backward question mark. The head of Taurus the bull makes a *V.* And the herdsman named *Boötes* (boh-OH-teez) looks more like a giant kite.

Constellations and asterisms look the way they do only because you look at them from the Earth. If you could travel many trillions of miles into space, you would see the star groupings change completely.

Perhaps someday people will travel the spaces between the stars and see how the constellations change. They might even come up with new constellations and asterisms that no one has ever thought of before.

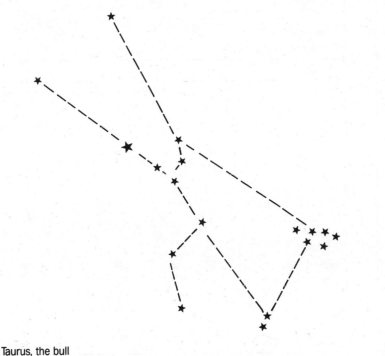

Taurus, the bull

Boötes, the herdsman

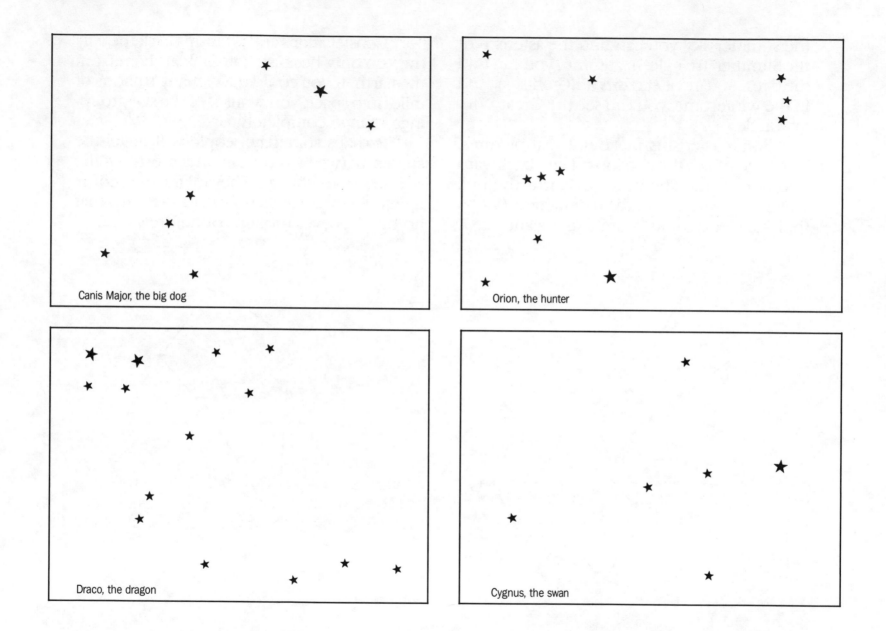

Canis Major, the big dog

Orion, the hunter

Draco, the dragon

Cygnus, the swan

Fun with the Zodiac

In ancient days, people believed that the planets were gods. They also believed that events on Earth could be predicted from the position of the stars. This belief is known as astrology (as-TROL-O-gee).

Centuries ago, astrology and astronomy became separate. Astronomy became a science in which people learn how things in the universe work. It changes as astronomers make new discoveries. Astrology is the same system of belief that existed thousands of years ago. Today we know that the planets are not gods. They cannot make things happen on Earth.

Today, people who believe that they can tell the future by the positions of the planets are called astrologers. Astrologers have given a name to the imaginary band of stars and constellations through which our sun, moon, and planets appear to travel. They call this band the zodiac (ZO-dee-ak). Astrologers divide this band into 12 equal parts (called signs), each one bearing the name of a constellation. Astrologers believe that you can tell what kind of person you will be by studying the position of the sun (your "sign") at the time you were born. They even try to predict your future in the newspaper! These predictions are called your horoscope (HOR-o-skope).

For example, If you were born on November 17, an astrologer would call you a "Scorpio." But the sun didn't appear in the direction of the constellation of Scorpius when you were born—unless you were born thousands of years ago. That's because the sky has changed since the time astrology began. If you were born on November 17, the sun really appeared against the constellation Libra!

The sun appears to pass through some constellations that aren't part of the zodiac. Between about November 30 and December 14, the sun appears in the constellation astronomers call Ophiuchus. Does this make you an Ophiuchan? Around March 13 and 14, the sun is in both Pisces *and* Cetus! What does *that* say about your future?

Astrology entertains many people, but it's the science of astronomy that provides accurate information about our universe. You can have fun with astrology, but remember that astronomy is the true science of the stars.

"Zodiac" Constellation	Dates in Horoscope	Dates When Sun is *Really* in Constellation
Aquarius (a-KWAIR-ee-us), the water-bearer	Jan. 20–Feb. 18	Feb. 15–Mar. 10
Pisces (PI-seez), the fish	Feb. 19–Mar. 20	Mar. 11–Apr. 17
Pisces and Cetus (SEE-tus)	—	Mar. 13 and 14
Aries (AIR-eez), the ram	Mar. 21–Apr. 19	Apr. 18–May 12
Taurus (TAW-rus), the bull	Apr. 20–May 20	May 13–June 20
Gemini (JEM-i-neye), the twins	May 21–June 20	June 21–July 19
Cancer (KAN-sur), the crab	June 21–July 22	July 20–Aug. 8
Leo (LEE-o), the lion	July 23–Aug. 22	Aug. 9–Sept. 15
Virgo (VER-go), the maiden	Aug. 23–Sept. 22	Sept. 15–Oct. 29
Libra (LEE-bra), the scales	Sept. 23–Oct. 22	Oct. 30–Nov. 21
Scorpius (SKOR-pee-us), the scorpion	Oct. 23–Nov. 21	Nov. 22–Nov. 29
Ophiuchus (o-fee-YOU-kus)	—	Nov. 30–Dec. 14
Sagittarius (saj-it-TA-ree-us), the archer	Nov. 22–Dec. 21	Dec. 15–Jan. 17
Capricornus (kap-ri-KORN-us), the she-goat	Dec. 22–Jan. 19	Jan. 18–Feb. 14

CHAPTER FIVE

Round and Round We Go

Look around you. You probably think you're sitting still, don't you? Compared to the room you're in, you're not moving at all. But to the sun and stars, you're moving very fast.

From the time you wake up to the time you get to school, you travel thousands of miles through space. You can't feel yourself moving because the Earth is so big beneath you. But you can see its motion when you look at the sky.

Our Rotating Earth

One of our Earth's motions is called "rotation" (roe-TAY-shun). That's what you do when you stand in one spot and turn around. When you rotate, you always turn around an "axis" (AKS-iss). This is an imaginary line that runs from your head to your feet.

Our Earth rotates once each day. Its axis runs through the planet from the North Pole to the South Pole. So when the Earth turns, it turns from west to east. This is why you see the sun rise in the east, pass high overhead at noontime, and set in the west each evening.

To see how this works, ask a friend to stand still and point a flashlight at you. Imagine the flashlight is the sun and you are the Earth, with your "north pole" at the top of your head.

Now face away from the flashlight and begin turning slowly from right to left. What happens to the flashlight as you turn? First it "rises" on your left side, passes in front of you, and "sets" on your right. It seems to move around *you* in the opposite direction, just like the sun!

Of course you know what's happening because you can feel yourself turning. But the

Earth person

Sun person

first face away from the flashlight
then turn slowly from right to left

Earth is so large beneath you that you can't feel it move. That's why people long ago believed that our world stood still, and that the sun went around *us*. It sure looks like it, doesn't it?

Of course, the Earth doesn't stop rotating when it gets dark. If you watch carefully at night, you'll see that the stars move, too. They seem to rise in the east, move across the sky, and set in the west just like the sun.

Let's go back to our experiment again. This time, imagine that you are the Earth, and everything else in the room is a star—the chairs, tables, windows, and ceilings. As you turn slowly, you will see that "stars" rise on your left side, pass in front of you, and set on your right just like the "sun."

But not all of these "stars" seem to "rise" and "set." Try the experiment again, but this time look over your head as you turn. What happens to the "star" straight over your "north pole?" It doesn't seem to move at all. And all the other nearby "stars" seem to go in circles around it. None of them "rise" or "set," either.

The stars you see at night do the same thing because the world is turning from west to east at a thousand miles an hour. Since the Earth is turning, everything in the sky seems to move toward the west.

turn from right to left
keep your eyes on an object on the ceiling

You can predict how the sun and stars will travel. To do this, go outdoors at night and look toward the south. Now sight a star behind a tree branch or telephone pole. If you return to that same spot one hour later, you will discover that the star has moved toward the west. If you keep watching that star, it will eventually set in the west.

But not all stars move like this, remember? One star sits right over the North Pole of Earth. Its name is Polaris. We also know it as the North Star.

The North Star never seems to move, so you can always see it in the same place. That makes it handy to people who are lost on a clear, dark night. If you see the North Star, you are facing north. South is behind you, east is on your right, and west is on your left.

During the night, all the stars near Polaris seem to turn around it. These are called "circumpolar" (sur-cum-POH-lar) stars because they seem to circle the "pole." The stars of the Big Dipper are circumpolar stars, so they can always be seen in the sky near Polaris.

Our Revolving Earth

There's another motion that our Earth has. It's called "revolution" (reh-voh-LOO-shun). This is what you do when you move around something else.

Our Earth revolves around the sun once each year. It moves at a speed of more than 66,000 miles per hour. This means that each day you travel *a million and a half* miles. And before you entered kindergarten, you traveled more than two billion miles through space!

As we move around the sun, the sky seems to change from season to season. It's just like riding a merry-go-round: As we go around, we look out in different directions.

Rotation and Revolution of the Earth

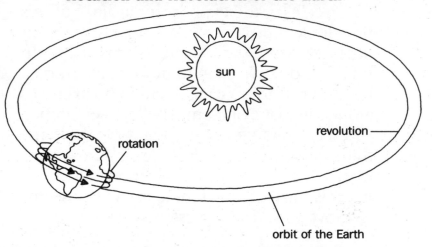

sun

rotation

revolution

orbit of the Earth

The Earth moves in the same way. As we circle the sun each year, we look out into space in different directions. That's why we see the stars of Scorpius in the summer and the stars of Orion in the winter.

Changes in the sky caused by revolution are harder to watch than those caused by rotation because they happen so slowly. If you're patient you can see them.

Go outdoors after dark and face east. Watch as a bright star rises behind the edge of a distant rooftop. Tomorrow night, go out and stand in *exactly* the same spot. If it's clear, you should see the star rise about four minutes earlier. The next night, it will rise four minutes earlier still.

After just two weeks, the star will rise an hour earlier than it did the first night. You'll see new stars rising beneath it.

Little by little, the sky changes as the Earth orbits the sun. Each night, we look outward in a slightly different direction. This is why we need a different sky map for each season of the year.

CHAPTER SIX

Where's the Moon Tonight?

Thousands of years ago, there was a man in China named Wan Ho who wanted very badly to go to the moon.

One day, Wan Ho waited for the moon to come up in the sky. He strapped himself into a chair and had his assistants place a catapult beneath him.

When he gave the command, his assistants let go and there was a huge flash. When the dust settled,

Wan Ho was gone, and so was his chair. No one ever saw him again.

The Chinese have a legend that the unfortunate Wan Ho actually made it to the moon. And in the dark patterns we see there, we can find him still sitting on his chair reading a book.

When you look at the moon shining brightly overhead, you can see all kinds of pictures in its markings—the face of a man, a woman wearing a diamond necklace, or even Bugs Bunny!

Today we know that these dark markings are flat, dry areas of lava that once flowed from inside the moon, cooled, and turned solid. But people didn't always know this.

Long ago, people saw these gray areas and thought they might be oceans and lakes. They even gave them names such as Ocean of Storms, Lake of Dreams, Bay of Rainbows.

The dark area that marks the face of Bugs Bunny is called the Sea of Tranquility (tran-KWIL-it-ee). This is where astronauts first landed on the moon in 1969.

If you watch the moon

The pull of the moon's gravity helps to change the tides of the oceans on Earth.

from night to night, you can see that its shape seems to change. Sometimes the moon looks like a banana, sometimes like the letter *D,* and sometimes like a giant round cookie. Whatever shape the moon has is called its "phase" (FAYZ).

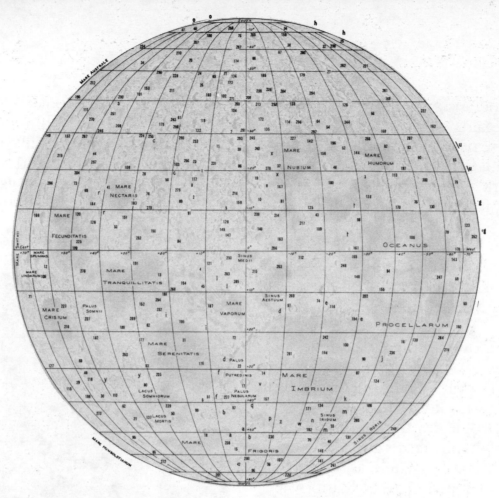

Astronomers have given Latin names to the mountains, valleys, and open areas of the moon that we can see from Earth. The flat open sections of the moon are called "maria," or seas. Although they are dry, they remind us of the open areas of our own planet that are covered by water. Here are some of the oceans, seas, lakes, and marshes for you to find on the map of the moon. Can you figure out what the names of the other maria stand for?

Mare Tranquillitatis (Sea of Tranquility)
Mare Serenitatis (Sea of Serenity)
Mare Vaporum (Sea of Vapors)
Mare Nubium (Sea of Clouds)
Mare Nectaris (Sea of Nectar)
Mare Spumans (Sea of Foam)
Palus Nebularum (Marsh of Mists)
Mare Australe (Southern Sea)
Oceanus Procellarum (Ocean of Storms)
Lacus Somniorum (Lake of Dreams)

U.S. astronauts have visited the moon six times. They collected rocks and other materials for scientific study.

One Moon, Many Faces

The moon doesn't really change its shape. It just looks that way from here because sunlight shines on it differently as the moon goes around the Earth.

Let's try an experiment to see how this works.

Go outdoors at night with a friend and take along a ball and a flashlight. The ball will represent the moon, and the flashlight will represent the sun. You will be the Earth.

Hold the ball in front of you and ask your friend to aim the flashlight toward it. Now stand with the ball in the direction of the light. You will notice it's hard to see the ball. That's because the light is shining on its other side.

Now keep the ball in front of you and move it slowly around you from right to left. The shape of the ball will seem to change. Before long, the lighted side will look like a banana. When the moon looks like this, we call it a "crescent" (KREH-sent) moon.

As you move the ball around you, you can see more and more of the lighted side. Soon, the ball will have the shape of the letter *D*, with its right-hand side lit up. When the moon looks like this, it's called a "first quarter" moon because you see one-quarter of its surface.

Keep moving the ball around you and it will seem to get bigger and bigger. This is what we call a "gibbous" (GIH-bus) phase.

When the ball is opposite the flashlight,

you see a round shape. This is what we call a "full" moon.

If you keep moving the ball around you, the moon will go from gibbous to last quarter and back to crescent. But now the phases will all appear backward. Finally our "moon-ball" moves toward the light again. This is called a "new" moon because a new cycle is beginning.

As you move the ball, you will notice that you can often see the moon-ball and the sun-flashlight in the sky together. The only time you can't is when the moon is full. That's because you must face away from the sun to see the full moon.

In your experiment, you can move your moon-ball around you in just a few minutes. But the Earth's moon takes about 28 days to circle the Earth. That means that we can see all its phases in just four weeks.

New moon

Start with the moon-ball directly in front of you

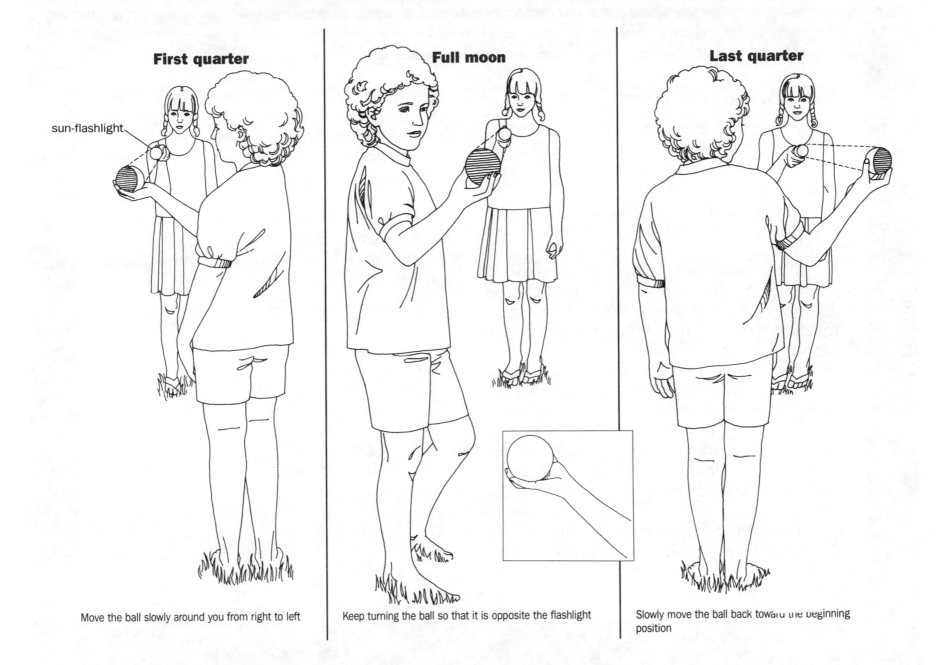

First quarter

sun-flashlight

Move the ball slowly around you from right to left

Full moon

Keep turning the ball so that it is opposite the flashlight

Last quarter

Slowly move the ball back toward the beginning position

Let's Make Craters

Some astronomers study the moon's craters by dropping rocks onto several types of dirt to see what kinds of holes are made. You can do the same experiment.

You'll need a place outside to do your experiment, a large pan or bucket, some water, and lots of dirt.

First, make some mud in the pan. It shouldn't be thin and runny, but thick and gooey mud—kind of like wet peanut butter. Imagine that the mud is the surface of the moon a long time ago.

Now you're ready to make some craters.

Stand up and hold a little mud in your fingers. When you drop it onto your "mud-moon," does anything happen? If not, try a larger lump. If still nothing happens, mix a little more water into the mud, but don't make it too wet. Keep trying until you make some nice craters.

Drop little lumps and big lumps. Try dropping them straight down and throwing them gently from the side. You can make all different kinds of craters—big ones and small ones, round ones and oval ones. Some might have a little "mountain" in the middle. And some craters might form inside other craters.

When you're finished, study a picture of the moon to see if you can find craters like yours. You can even use a flashlight to light your craters from different angles and see how their shadows change.

You're on your way to becoming a lunar astronomer!

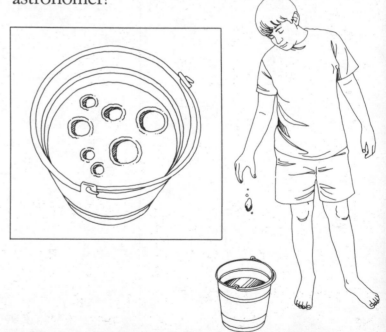

Moon craters are formed by meteorites and other space debris hitting the moon's surface at speeds of thousands of miles per hour.

CHAPTER SEVEN

Shadow Games

Pretend you are a shepherd of long ago, standing in the fields tending your flock. Slowly the sun disappears. The sky darkens and the wind begins to blow. Stars come out in the middle of the day, and an eerie glow comes from where the sun used to be.

What has happened? Are the gods angry? What can you do to make them happy again?

For ages, this kind of event was very scary to people. Today we know not to be afraid of such a sight. We

A total solar eclipse. The glow around the darkened moon is called the sun's corona.

know it happens whenever a new moon passes in front of the sun and blocks it from view. We call it a "total solar eclipse" (SO-lar ee-KLIPS). An eclipse happens when one object hides another object.

When Noon Turns to Night

In the days before solar eclipses were understood, they were believed to be warnings from the gods. Some believed that the sun was being eaten by a huge dragon, so they stood outside and beat drums to scare off the monster. After a while, the sky would brighten, the sun would return, and everyone felt proud that they had driven away the evil monster and saved the sun.

Centuries ago, astronomers figured out that the "monster" was just the moon. They could even predict when the next eclipse would be. This was important to kings and emperors of long ago, because they could use the knowledge of eclipses to scare people.

One story tells of two ancient Chinese astronomers named Hi and Ho who predicted a solar eclipse in 2137 B.C. They were so excited that they forgot to tell the emperor. While they were laughing and rolling in the street, the sky darkened, and the emperor became furious that he had not been told. He ordered the two astronomers' heads chopped off as punishment. Luckily, that doesn't happen today!

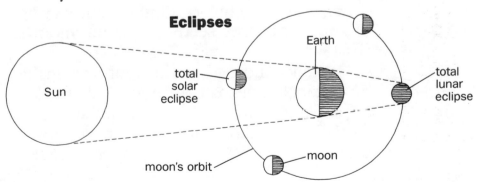

51 ○ Shadow Games ○ 51

Eclipses of the sun have changed the course of history. In 840 A.D., Emperor Louis of Bavaria was so frightened that he died during a five-minute solar eclipse. After his death, his sons fought over his empire and later divided the land into the countries we know today as France, Germany, and Italy.

A total eclipse of the sun is nothing to be afraid of. It happens when the moon passes in front of the sun and blocks it from view. This lets us see the faint, silvery atmosphere of the sun called the corona (coh-ROH-na). It shines for a few minutes while the moon blocks the sun, and then disappears as the moon continues on its journey.

From any one place on Earth, total eclipses of the sun are so rare that astronomers must often travel very far to see them.

An annular eclipse is a total eclipse that occurs when the moon appears very small and doesn't completely block out the sun. A ring of sunlight can be seen around the moon's shadow.

A much more common event is when the moon blocks only part of the sun. This is called a "partial solar eclipse." You can usually see a partial solar eclipse from your home town every few years. When this happens, the sky doesn't become very dark, and if astronomers didn't tell us it was coming, most people would never notice.

A solar eclipse is fun to watch, but can be very dangerous. **NEVER LOOK DIRECTLY AT THE SUN, BECAUSE IT CAN BLIND YOU IN ONLY AN INSTANT.** Don't even try to look at the sun through several pieces of black film, or smoked glass—these are just as dangerous.

One safe way to watch a solar eclipse is to make a sun projector. With a pencil or paper punch, poke a ¼-inch hole into a piece of black cardboard or paper. Put the hole over the middle of a small mirror and go outside in the sunlight. Use the covered mirror to catch the sun's light and shine it onto a piece of white paper a few feet away. This is the image of

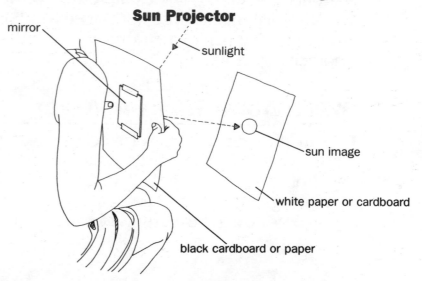

Sun Projector

mirror

sunlight

sun image

white paper or cardboard

black cardboard or paper

the sun. Now you and your friends or family can all watch the eclipse together and be totally safe.

If you make the hole bigger, the image will be brighter but will become fuzzy. If you make the hole smaller, the image will become sharper but will be fainter.

The Earth's Shadow

Another kind of eclipse is perfectly safe to watch. This is an eclipse of the moon, or lunar eclipse. It occurs not at the time of new moon, but at the time of full moon.

A lunar eclipse occurs when the moon moves into the shadow of the Earth. When you watch a lunar eclipse, you'll see the round shadow of the Earth on the moon's surface. It seems to pass from east to west across the moon's face. But remember, it's the moon that's moving through the shadow in the opposite direction, from west to east!

If the moon moves only partly through the shadow, you'll see a partial lunar eclipse. But if it enters the shadow completely, it's called a total lunar eclipse. Total eclipses of the moon aren't as rare as total solar eclipses because they can be seen from a much wider area of our planet. They can also look very weird. Because they can sometimes make the moon look blood-red, they used to scare people.

Today, eclipses are fun to watch, and you don't need a telescope to see them. The next time an eclipse appears in your city, why not ask your friends, family, and neighbors to join you for an eclipse party?

A partial lunar eclipse filmed over a period of time above New York City.

Upcoming Eclipses

CAUTION: Never look directly at the sun! It can blind you in only an instant! Safe ways to view the sun (such as using a sun projector) can be found on pages 52 and 71.

An annular eclipse (AN-you-lar ee-KLIPS) is an eclipse of the sun in which a ring of the sun appears to surround the smaller, darker moon.

Solar Eclipses

Date	Type of eclipse	Where to see it
July 11, 1991	Total	Partial eclipse in U.S.and Canada
January 4, 1992	Annular	Partial eclipse on West Coast of U.S.
May 21, 1993	Partial	North and Western U.S., all of Canada
May 10, 1994	Annular	NE to SW U.S.; partial eclipse in rest of U.S. and Canada
April 29, 1995	Annular	Partial from the southern tip of Florida

Lunar Eclipses

Date	Type of eclipse	Where to see it
August 6, 1990	Partial	The beginning visible only in western parts of the U.S. and Canada
December 21, 1991	Partial	All of U.S. and Canada
June 15, 1992	Partial	All of U.S. and Canada
December 9, 1992	Total	The ending visible only in eastern parts of the U.S. and Canada
June 4, 1993	Total	The beginning visible only in western parts of the U.S. and Canada
November 29, 1993	Total	All of U.S. and Canada
May 25, 1994	Partial	All of U.S. and Canada
April 15, 1995	Partial	Eastern parts of the U.S. and Canada

CHAPTER EIGHT

Unexpected Visitors

Imagine standing outdoors on a clear, dark night watching the stars and planets overhead. Suddenly, the heavens are split by a bright flash of light. Then, moments later, it's gone.

What was that? Did one of the stars fall from the sky? Most people call these "falling stars" or "shooting stars." Astronomers know them as "meteors" (MEE-tee-ohrs).

Skywatchers of old saw them, too. They believed that meteors were flashes of light high in the atmosphere of Earth. Even the word *meteor* comes from the Greek language and means "something in the air."

Today we know that the ancients were right. Shooting stars aren't stars at all. They are specks of cosmic dust that collide with our atmosphere many miles up.

The largest meteorite in a museum, the Cape York Meteorite "Ahnighito" can be seen at the Hayden Planetarium of the American Museum of Natural History in New York City.

Stones from Heaven

As the Earth moves through space, it passes millions of particles of rock and iron called "meteoroids." Occasionally one strikes our atmosphere at tens of miles per second. Friction with the air heats it to thousands of degrees Fahrenheit, and the meteoroid burns up in an instant.

When a meteoroid collides with our atmosphere at night it is called a meteor. You might see its fiery death as a brilliant burst of light. But no matter how spectacular they

A meteor flashes by the Little Dipper (at right) on a warm summer night.

seem, most meteors are just specks of dust smaller than a grain of sand. We see them only because they burn so brightly.

These unexpected visitors are called "sporadic" meteors. On any clear, dark night you may be able to see one streak across the sky every 15 or 20 minutes.

You can see meteors in many brightnesses and colors. Some can smoke or break into pieces. Some can create a whistling sound or even explode. These are called fireballs or "bolides" (BOW-lieds).

Sometimes our air collides with a rock or piece of iron large enough to survive its plunge to Earth and crash to the ground. It is then called a meteorite" (MEE-tee-ohr-ite).

You can see meteorites on display in planetariums and science museums. Most are small chunks of iron or stone that look like normal Earth rocks. But others are huge boulders that weigh hundreds or thousands of pounds. One of the largest meteorites ever found is on display at the American Museum/Hayden Planetarium in New York. It weighs more than 34 tons.

When rocks this big fall, they can do much damage. One chunk of iron as big as a house fell to Earth about 50,000 years ago in what is now northern Arizona. It ripped open

Meteor Crater in Arizona is more than 4,000 feet wide and 570 feet deep.

a hole we call Meteor Crater.

Luckily, collisions with rocks from space are rare. Only about 2,000 meteorites have been found around the world.

Long ago, these "stones from heaven" were thought to be sacred by some American Indians. Meteorites were wrapped in mummy cloth and buried with valuable possessions.

In 1492—the year Columbus made his famous voyage—a meteorite fell to the ground in a small town in France. It was displayed in a church for all the town's peasants to worship.

Today, astronomers study these space rocks to learn about other worlds of our solar system. They now think that meteorites might be pieces of asteroids that fell to Earth. Some that have been found on the ice fields of Antarctica may be pieces of the moon or Mars, blasted into space millions of years ago. Some might even be pieces of passing comets.

The comet "Bennett" has a tail millions of miles long.

A Cosmic Litterbug

Comets are chunks of ice and dust that orbit the sun in a giant swarm out near the edge of our solar system. These "dirty snowballs" cannot be seen with even the world's largest telescopes. But sometimes one is tugged inward by the gravity of the sun or the planets and rushes past the Earth.

As a comet nears the sun, some of its ice evaporates, and its gas and dust is blown away by the sun's radiation—forming its long and beautiful tail. It's this tail that we can sometimes see in the sky.

Unlike meteors, comets don't streak across our sky. Instead, they drift slowly and silently through the stars from night to night.

Some comets visit our neighborhood only once. They speed past Earth on their way to interstellar space and are never seen again. Others—like Halley's (HAL-eez) Comet—return now and then, and may even appear several times in one's life. The next time you'll be able to see Halley's Comet in the night sky will be in the year 2061.

Each time a comet rounds the sun, some of its material is blown into space. The comet scatters this debris along its path, and becomes a sort of cosmic litterbug.

As our Earth journeys around the sun, we cross these swarms of dust at certain times each year. When we do, we can see showers of meteors—all appearing to fall from one part of the sky.

Meteor showers are named for the constellation from which the meteors seem to fall. Perhaps the most famous is the *Perseid* (PER-see-id) shower every mid-August. During this shower you can often see dozens of meteors every hour, all seeming to come from the constellation Perseus.

Sometimes a meteor shower can be even more spectacular. For a short while on the evening of November 17, 1966, stargazers watched as the heavens opened and more than 2,000 meteors fell every minute!

Meteors and meteor showers are exciting to watch, and you don't need binoculars or a telescope to see them. All you need is a clear, dark night, a lounge chair to lie on, and a blanket or sleeping bag to keep warm. The rest will be done by Mother Nature!

This imaginative woodcut shows a meteor shower off of Cape Florida in 1799.

Major Meteor Showers

Best Viewing Dates	Shower Name	Best Time to View	Direction to Look	Average Number Each Hour
January 3–5	Quadrantids	4–6 A.M.	North	40–150
April 21–23	Lyrids	3–5 A.M.	South	10–15
May 3–5	Eta Aquarids	3–5 A.M.	Southeast	10–40
July 26–30	Delta Aquarids	1–3 A.M.	South	10–35
August 11–13	Perseids	3–5 A.M.	Northeast	50–100
October 20–22	Orionids	3–5 A.M.	South	10–70
November 15–17	Leonids	4–6 A.M.	South	5–20
December 13–15	Geminids	1–3 A.M.	South	50–80

Collecting Micrometeorites

What happens to a bright meteor after it burns up in our sky? It turns to ashes.

These ashes float through the atmosphere and eventually fall to the ground. Rain or snow can help "wash" much of this meteoric dust out of the air.

About 10,000 tons of meteoric dust falls to Earth every day. Each piece is so small that you need a magnifying glass or microscope to see it.

You can collect meteoric dust for yourself. Put a large container (such as a bucket) outdoors and collect several gallons of rainwater or melted snow. Then bring the water inside and let it evaporate until only a pint or two is left.

Next, pass a strong magnet through the water. You should pick up tiny pieces of metal dust. Place these tiny scrapings from the magnet on a sheet of glass and look at them under a microscope or magnifying glass. You'll be surprised by the number and shapes of the particles.

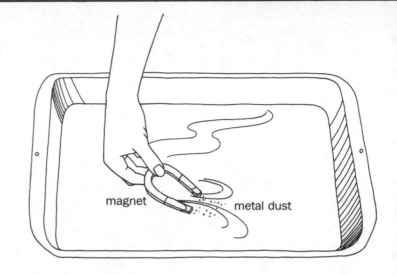

magnet   metal dust

If you live in or near a large city, some of these particles might be pollution from nearby factories. But if you live in the country, most will be meteoric dust from space.

CHAPTER NINE

How Far Can I See?

Did you ever wonder how far you could see?

On the Earth, we can see pretty far. If our world were as smooth as ice we could see things on the horizon several miles away before our round planet curves out of sight.

But our world isn't so smooth. Mountains, forests, and buildings stick up from the land. So, on a good, clear day, we might be able to see distant mountaintops—perhaps 50 miles away.

Spiral galaxies such as this one contain billions of stars.

If you want to see even farther, all you have to do is look upward into the sky. Up there, the nearest object you can see is the moon.

If you could magically ride your bicycle to the moon, it would take nearly two years to get there—even peddling as fast as you could without stopping to rest!

Yet our moon is our nearest neighbor in space—240,000 miles away. That's a quarter of a million miles! Everything else is farther still. Our sun is 93 *million* miles away. And the stars we see at night are *trillions* of miles away.

The stars are so far away that it takes a while for their light to get here. Light travels at an incredible speed—about 186,000 miles every second. This is so fast that if you had a flashlight powerful enough, its beam could go completely around the Earth seven and one-half times in just one second!

Looking Back into Time

Because light moves so quickly, we on Earth normally see things at nearly the same time they happen. But when we look into space, it's a different story.

Light takes a long time to travel the vast distances across the universe. For example, look at our moon. Light from our nearest cosmic neighbor takes nearly one and a half seconds to cross a quarter-million miles of space.

Sunlight takes eight minutes to get here. That means that if there were an explosion on the sun, you'd see it eight minutes after it happened. It takes that long for the sun's light to reach our eyes. In other words, by looking into space we can look straight into the past! And the farther you look, the farther back into time you can see.

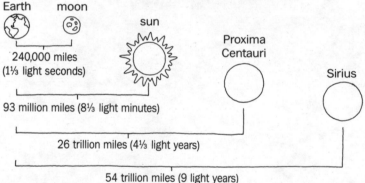

Distances in Light-Years

Earth   moon   sun   Proxima Centauri   Sirius

240,000 miles (1⅓ light seconds)

93 million miles (8⅓ light minutes)

26 trillion miles (4⅓ light years)

54 trillion miles (9 light years)

The nearest star beyond the sun is called Proxima Centauri. It's about 26 trillion miles away (that's 26,000,000,000,000!). The farthest galaxies may be a hundred million trillion miles away (1 with 20 zeros after it)!

These numbers are so big that astronomers can't even imagine them. They discovered that measuring distances to stars in miles is about as silly as measuring the distance from your home to your school in inches!

So astronomers invented a larger measurement of distance to replace the mile called a "light-year." One light-year is the distance that light travels in one year—about six trillion miles. This is how we measure star distances.

The bright wintertime star *Sirius* (SEE-ree-us) lies some 54 trillion miles away. Its light that we see now left Sirius nine years ago, and has been traveling through space ever since. So we say that Sirius is nine light-years away. In other words, we see Sirius as it was nine years ago.

But Sirius is one of the *nearest* of our nighttime stars. Most are much farther away. For example, the brightest star in the Big Dipper, *Dubhe* (DUH-bee), lies a hundred light-years away. And we see the summertime star Deneb as *it* was 1500 years ago.

It works backward, too. Imagine astronomers on a planet orbiting Sirius. If they could look toward Earth with a super-powerful telescope, they would see us as we were nine years ago. What could they be watching right now?

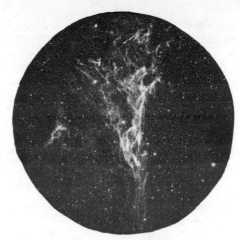

This nebula contains material from an exploding star or "supernova."

Astronomers at Deneb would see the Earth as it was 1500 years ago—near the end of the fourth century. They could be watching the fall of the Roman Empire right now!

As far as these distances seem, your eyes can see much farther. If you look near the northeastern corner of the Square of Pegasus on a really dark night, you might see a faint, fuzzy patch of light called the Great Galaxy in Andromeda. (To find the galaxy of Andromeda, see the fall star map on page 27.)

This galaxy is a twin of our own Milky Way and lies some two million light-years away. That means that the light which strikes our eyes began its journey toward Earth two million years ago—long before human beings walked the planet Earth.

Believe it or not, we can see even farther! But for this, our eyes will need some help.

Cosmic Distances

OBJECT	DISTANCE (Light-years)	CONSTELLATION
Sirius	9	Canis Major (the big dog)
Altair	16	Aquila (the eagle)
Arcturus	34	Boötes (the herdsman)
Regulus	69	Leo (the lion)
Dubhe	100	Ursa Major (the great bear)
Spica	220	Virgo (the maiden)
Pleiades Cluster	410	Taurus (the bull)
Polaris	820	Ursa Minor (the little bear)
Alphirk	1000	Cepheus (the king)
Deneb	1500	Cygnus (the swan)
Al Anz	2800	Auriga (the charioteer)
Andromeda Galaxy	2,000,000	Andromeda (the daughter of Cassiopeia)

Measuring the Sky

Astronomers estimate sizes and positions in the sky with a unit called a "degree" (dee-GREE). They use advanced measuring equipment to make precise calculations. To get an idea of how to use this measurement, stretch your arm out in front of you. Now, hold up your little finger and close one eye to focus on your finger. Your finger's thickness measures about one degree. The thickness of your fist will appear to be about 10 degrees. If you open your hand, the distance from your little finger to your thumb measures about 15 degrees. You can use these "measuring sticks" to estimate distances between objects.

If you want to describe how high something is above the horizon, use your fist or finger to measure upward from the horizon. This will tell you the object's height, or "altitude" (AL-tih-tood). If a bright star is about one fist's-width up from the horizon, you can help a friend locate the star by saying that its altitude is about 10 degrees.

(continued next page)

Close one eye and focus on your little finger

The measurement of an object's position to the left or right is called the "azimuth" (AZ-ih-muth). We can think of the horizon as a circle that surrounds us. Since a circle has 360 degrees, we can measure from one to 360. We always start at the north point on the horizon and measure eastward. A star in the northeast, has an azimuth at 45 degrees "east of north." A star due east is said to be 90 degrees "east of north." A star due south is 180 degrees "east of north."

Try describing the altitude and azimuth of the moon. You can watch the moon move from west to east around the Earth. Each night it moves through the stars about 12 degrees eastward. By using your hand to measure 12 degrees, you can predict where the moon will be from night to night. Remember, it might not be exact, but it should be close.

You can even describe how fast something appears to be moving. Suppose a satellite crosses the length of your outstretched fist in 5 seconds. All you have to do is divide the number of degrees measured by your fist (10) by the number of seconds (5) to get the satellite's speed of 2 degrees per second (10 degrees divided by 5 seconds).

CHAPTER TEN

Through the Looking Glass

Once you've made friends with the stars, you can take a closer look with an instrument called a telescope. Even a small telescope can help you see farther into space and can show you a remarkable universe far beyond your imagination.

There are two kinds of telescopes. One is called a "refractor" and the other a "reflector." A refractor has a lens to catch light and focus it into an image. A reflector uses a curved mirror to do the same thing.

A telescope with a lens or mirror two inches across is called a two-inch telescope. Most beginning stargazers start with a telescope two or four inches across. The biggest telescope in the world has a mirror 236 inches—or nearly 20 feet—across!

Many people think that astronomers use telescopes just to magnify images from space, but that's not true. Astronomers use telescopes to gather more light than our eyes can, just as a bucket can gather more rain than a drinking glass. For this reason, astronomers sometimes call telescopes "light buckets."

Telescopes have several parts. One, of course, is the lens or mirror. This is held in place by the telescope tube. The tube of a larger telescope is sometimes supported by a three-legged stand called a "tripod." All telescopes have eyepieces; these are magnifying lenses that make the image appear larger.

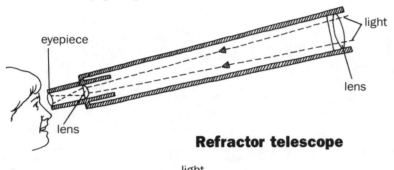

Refractor telescope

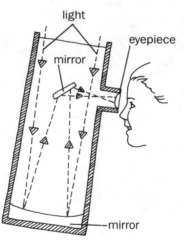

Reflector telescope

Using a "Light Bucket"

Before you use a telescope at night, try it in the daylight (Don't look at the sun!). This will help you learn to use it.

First aim your telescope at an object on the ground and focus to make sure the image is sharp. When you first look through your telescope, don't be surprised to find that everything looks upside down. All telescopes turn things upside down. But when you look at the sky, it really doesn't matter. After all, there's no up or down in space!

Practice aiming the telescope at distant

trees or mountains, and practice moving and focusing it. Look through each eyepiece, and learn which ones give the best image. If you have a tripod, make sure it's strong and that it stands on level ground, for even a little wind will bounce it around.

If you have a larger telescope that has a sun filter, you might like to try looking at our nearest star.

BUT WAIT! NEVER LOOK AT THE SUN THROUGH YOUR TELESCOPE—EVEN WITH YOUR SUN FILTER. The sun's light and heat are so strong that they can crack your filter and blind you instantly.

There is one safe way to view the sun—project the sun's image onto a piece of white cardboard. Without looking through your telescope, point it up toward the sun. Now watch the shadow of the telescope tube on the ground. It will probably look like an egg or a stretched circle. As you move the telescope, the shadow will change. When the tube's shadow becomes a small circle, it means that the sun's light is shining straight down the tube.

Now hold a piece of white cardboard behind the eyepiece and you should see a bright image of the sun projected onto it. (You might have to wiggle the telescope a bit to get

View the Sun Safely

telescope

sharpen the image of the sun

white cardboard

the sun's image to appear.) Now focus the edge of the sun until it is sharp. This is the best and safest way to view the sun.

You might notice that the sun has dark spots on it. These are called "sunspots." Sunspots are huge magnetic storms in the hot gas of the sun. Some are even larger than our Earth.

If you sketch the sunspots from day to day, you'll discover that they move. This is because the sun rotates about once every 26 days. But when a sunspot disappears behind the sun, don't expect to see it again. Sunspots often change their shapes, and sometimes they disappear.

Once you've practiced during daylight, you're ready to turn your telescope toward the sky when darkness falls. But don't expect too much from your new telescope.

People often become disappointed when they look through a small telescope for the first time. They expect to see giant colorful planets and stars, swirling galaxies, and clouds of gas—just like they see in photographs.

But remember, these are photos taken with the world's biggest telescopes. Your telescope is much smaller, so the images you see will be much smaller as well. However, what you can see is more exciting than a photo because it's real.

Probably the first thing you'll want to look at is the moon. You can easily see craters, mountains, and flat plains of solid lava. Soon you'll discover that shadows on the moon change from night to night as the moon orbits the Earth. All the features of the moon have names, and a map of the moon such as the one on page 44 can help you discover them all for yourself.

You can study the moon's craters, mountains, and valleys with a telescope.

Before long you'll discover that your telescope magnifies not only the moon itself, but also its motion across the sky. You'll need to move your telescope once in a while to follow objects westward through the night.

Next you'll probably want to see the planets. Jupiter is perhaps the most fun to watch. You can see dark brown and red stripes crossing its face. Cloud bands stretch across the entire planet. Right next to Jupiter you'll see its four brightest moons. Their names are *Io* (EYE-oh), *Europa* (you-ROH-puh), *Ganymede* (GAN-ee-meed), and *Callisto* (cuh-LIS-toe). They look like four tiny stars in a straight line. What is most remarkable is that you can see them move from night to night—sometimes even from hour to hour! Occasionally one travels in front of, or behind, the planet. When this happens, you can see only three of the moons. Try sketching their positions every clear night.

Another fascinating planet is Venus. You won't see any features on this world because Venus is covered with thick white clouds. But Venus does show phases just like the moon. Sometimes you'll see it as a tiny, "full" Venus, and several months later as a larger, thin crescent.

Saturn is probably everyone's favorite planet. Saturn appears as a tiny dot surrounded by bright rings. Even through a small telescope, these rings are a spectacular sight. But Saturn's rings are so thin that every 15 years they line up and seem to disappear from our view. The next time this will happen is in 1996.

A montage of photos taken by a Voyager spacecraft near Jupiter (lower left) and four of its moons. These moons—Io, Europa, Ganymede, and Callisto—are called the Galilean satellites.

Beyond the Planets

Stars can be found farther out in space. When you aim your telescope toward a star, you'll discover that it still looks like a tiny point of light. The stars are so far away that even the world's biggest telescopes can't magnify them.

But looking at star "clusters" is something very different. These stars are grouped together in families of dozens, hundreds, or even thousands of stars.

Aim your telescope toward the bright cluster called the Pleiades. Here you will see dozens of bright bluish-white stars together in space. The Pleiades may be a family of young stars all born together only a few hundred million years ago.

On a dark night, you might see the great round star cluster in Hercules as a faint smudge of light. With a telescope, you may be able to see it as a group of hundreds or thousands of stars packed together in a ball. This family of stars is one of the oldest in our galaxy and lies some 21,000 light-years away.

Aim your telescope toward other smudges of light found around the sky and you might see a cloud of glowing gas called a *nebula* (NEB-yoo-luh). Perhaps the most famous is the Great Orion Nebula, just below the belt of Orion, the hunter. This cloud is a nursery where stars are being born. They collapse from the gas and dust inside the cloud and heat up until they begin to glow. This nebula is lit up by four newborn stars right in its middle. These stars are called the "Trapezium" (tra-PEE-zee-um).

Beyond the stars lie the galaxies. These are not very easy to see because they are so faint and far away. But if you know just where to look, you can see many.

The most famous, of course, is the Great Andromeda Galaxy. It appears in our telescope as a long haze of light. This twin of our Milky Way Galaxy shines with the light of a hundred billion stars, and lies two million light-years away.

Although a small telescope can give you a totally new look at the sky, you can also explore the night sky with a good pair of binoculars. These can help you to see many things invisible to your eyes alone, and can teach you what to look for with a telescope.

You might like to try making a telescope yourself. If there is a planetarium or amateur astronomy group in your area, call and ask about classes you can take or books you can read about building your own telescope (see Further Exploring, pages 85–89). Building a telescope is not easy, but it's a great way to learn how one really works.

CHAPTER ELEVEN

Becoming an Astronomer

The trees are swaying in the cool night air. Above us is a black sky, and the stars sparkle like diamonds.

Up here on the high mountaintop, the night is quiet. In the darkness, all we hear is the faint whirring of a motor, and the gentle ticking of a clock.

In front of us stands a huge structure. It's a telescope, lit only by faint, red light. The giant eye gazes outward like a great snowy owl in search of prey.

As we peer through the eyepiece, we see sights no human being has ever seen before. This is the exciting job of an astronomer.

Today's astronomers must know computers and electronics so they can work with giant telescopes and robot spacecraft. They must know optics (the study of light) to build bigger and better telescopes and cameras. They must know geology, weather, chemistry, physics, and biology to study other worlds—and sometimes even our own world.

Astronomers seldom work alone. They must be able to speak and write clearly to let

This satellite photograph shows Hurricane Allen on August 8, 1980. You can see the hurricane spiral in the Gulf of Mexico.

The Kitt Peak National Observatory near Tucson, Arizona.

The Space Shuttle Discovery during an engine test at Cape Canaveral, Florida.

others know of their discoveries. They must know a foreign language to talk with astronomers from other countries. And they must get along well with all kinds of people.

Most importantly, astronomers must know mathematics to figure out the secrets of the universe.

Many astronomers do their own research at colleges or universities. Some use telescopes or spacecraft, and some do experiments in laboratories. Some even become astronauts and journey into space.

Not all astronomers do research. Some teach at colleges and universities. Some write articles and books, and some work in science museums and planetariums to bring the excitement of the universe to other people.

An astronomer's job is becoming more exciting every day. Some say we are entering a time that future historians will know as the Golden Age of Astronomy. And each one of us can be a part of it.

The world's largest radio telescope has a collecting area of 1,000 feet across. It is located near the city of Arecibo, Puerto Rico. (Inset) Workers must keep the 18 acres of the reflecting dish in working order.

This is exciting work, and astronomers are paid to do it. But there aren't many jobs for professional astronomers, so people who hire them want only the very best. That's why astronomers must sometimes study more than eight years after high school before they can be hired.

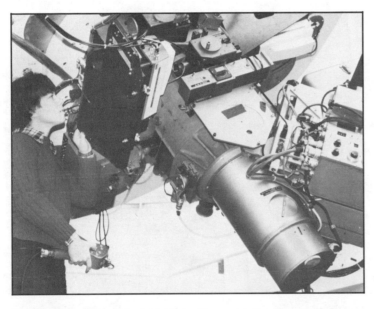

Some astronomers work in observatories. They watch the stars using high-powered telescopes like the one above.

Amateur Astronomers

You don't need to become a professional astronomer to study the universe. By day, some people work as teachers or plumbers or dentists or farmers. By night, they become astronomers as they gaze at the stars. They are called "amateur" (AM-ah-chur) astronomers because they aren't paid to study the heavens. They do it only because they enjoy it.

Amateur astronomers do many things. They search for comets and map the moon or planets. They photograph the sky and watch stars that change their brightnesses. They also help professional astronomers learn about the universe.

Thousands of amateur astronomers in this country have clubs, hold meetings, and talk about what they are studying. There might be an amateur astronomy group in your area or at your school. Check your phone book or call a library, planetarium, or college to find out how you can join.

Professional and amateur astronomers all share one thing in common: We are all curious about the universe in which we live, and we all try to learn more about it every day.

In reading this book and doing the activities, you have already become an astronomer. You are curious, you have observed the universe, and you have tried to understand what you have seen. Now you can go on to learn even more about astronomy.

Whatever path you choose—professional or amateur—the night sky will always be there. The stars will shine, the planets will move, meteors will flash by, and comets will come and go.

It's an exciting place—the night sky. You should never stop watching the sky, and you should never, ever stop asking questions about the beautiful and mysterious universe in which we live.

Glossary

Altitude (AL-tih-tood)   Height. In astronomy altitude is used to measure an object's position above the horizon.

Annular eclipse (AN-you-lur ee-KLIPS)   A total eclipse in which a ring of the sun appears to surround the smaller, darker moon.

Asterism (AS-tur-i-zum)   A group of stars that forms the outline of something familiar, such as the summer triangle. An asterism can be part of a constellation *See also* Constellation.

Asteroid (AS-tur-oyd)   A chunk of iron or rock that orbits the sun. Most asteroids orbit the sun between the orbits of Mars and Jupiter.

Astronomer (as-TRON-o-mur)   A scientist who studies the planets, stars, galaxies and clouds of dust and gas that make up our universe.

Aurora borealis (UH-rohr-uh bohr-ee-AL-is)   Colored lights in the northern sky caused by electrified gas particles from the sun hitting our atmosphere near the North Pole. Also known as the northern lights.

Averted (uh-VUR-ted) vision   Looking at something out of the side of your eyes while focusing them elsewhere; a trick that helps you to see very faint objects in the sky.

Axis (AKS-iss)   An imaginary line that passes through the North and South poles of the Earth.

Azimuth (AZ-ih-muth)   The measure of an object's position east and west around the horizon.

Billion (BIL-yun)   A large number represented by a 1 followed by nine zeros (1,000,000,000).

Bolide (BOW-lied)   A brilliant meteor that smokes, whistles, or explodes.

Circle   The shape that astronomers use to measure distances between stars, planets, satellites, and other objects in the sky. A circle is measured in 360 degrees, with north at 0 degrees, east at 90 degrees, south at 180 degrees, and west at 270 degrees.

Comet (KOM-et)   A chunk of ice that sometimes appears in our sky and shows a long, glowing stream of cosmic debris that looks like a tail.

Constellation (kahn-steh-LAY-shun)   A group of stars named for a person, thing, or animal. Astronomers use constellations to identify certain areas of the sky. *See also* Asterism.

Corona (coh-ROH-na)   The outer atmosphere of the sun that can be seen from Earth during a total eclipse of the sun.

Crater (KRAY-tur)   A hole in the surface of the Earth, the moon, or another solid object. These can be formed by a large rock falling from space.

Dark adapted (uh-DAPP-ted)   When your eyes have become adjusted to darkness.

Degree (dee-GREE)   A measurement equal to 1/360th of a circle. When you are measuring distances in the night sky, one degree is about the width of your little finger held at arm's length.

Eclipse. *See* Lunar eclipse; Solar eclipse.

Falling star. *See* Meteor.

Galaxy (GAL-ax-ee)   A collection of hundreds of billions of stars, clusters of stars, clouds of dust, and gas. Our Milky Way is a galaxy.

Globular cluster (GLOB-yoo-lar KLUSS-tur)   A tightly packed ball of thousands or millions of stars.

Gravity (GRAV-ih-tee)   The force that holds us on the Earth, keeps the moon around the Earth, and holds the Earth and planets around the sun.

Horizon (hoe-RYE-zun)   An imaginary line that divides the sky and the ground.

Light pollution   Light from street lights, billboards, and other sources that shines into the sky and makes it difficult to see faint stars.

Lunar eclipse (LU-nar ee-KLIPS)   When the moon passes into the shadow of the Earth and seems to disappear for a while.

Meteor (MEE-tee-ohr)   A speck of dust that burns as it falls into our atmosphere. Also called a falling star or shooting star.

Meteorite (MEE-tee-ohr-ite)   A chunk of iron or rock that has fallen to Earth from space.

Meteoroid (MEE-tee-ohr-oyd)   A piece of dust, rock, or iron tumbling through space.

Milky Way   The galaxy where we live. We see part of it as a hazy band of light in the night sky.

Million (MIL-yun)   A large number represented by a 1 followed by six zeros (1,000,000).

Nebula (NEB-yoo-lah)   A cloud of gas and dust in space.

Observatory (ob-ZUR-vuh-tohr-ee)   A place where astronomers use large telescopes to observe the sky.

Orbit (OHR-bit)   The path of an object that travels around another.

Phase (FAYZ)   The shape an object seems to have as the light falling on it changes.

Planet   A large body that travels around the sun and shines by reflecting sunlight. Nine planets can be found in our solar system.

Planetarium (plan-e-TAIR-ee-um)   A place where astronomers can project lights onto a round ceiling and create images of stars, planets, and galaxies.

Reflector telescope (ree-FLEK-tor TEL-e-scope)   A telescope that uses a mirror to gather light from the sky and focus it into an image.

Refractor telescope (ree-FRAK-tor TEL-e-scope)   A telescope that uses a lens to gather light from the sky and focus it into an image.

Revolution (reh-voh-LOO-shun)   The motion of one object moving around another object.

Rotation (roe-TAY-shun)   A spinning motion.

Satellite (SAT-uh-lite)   A natural or man-made object revolving around another object, such as a planet. Our moon is a natural satellite.

Shooting star. *See* Meteor.

Solar eclipse (SO-lar ee-KLIPS)   When the moon blocks out the light of the sun and casts its shadow onto the Earth.

Spiral Galaxy (SPY-ruhl GAL-ax-ee)   A galaxy in the shape of a pinwheel.

Star   A tiny point of light in the nighttime sky. Each star is a large, glowing ball of gas. Our sun is a nearby star.

Star cluster   A family of stars held together by gravity.

Starhopping   A trick astronomers use to find an object in the sky by using other stars as "pointers."

Sun   The large, glowing ball of gas that lights and warms our day and makes it possible for life to exist on Earth. The sun is a nearby star.

Sunspots   Dark spots on the face of the sun that appear to rotate with the sun.

Supernova (soo-per-NO-vah)   The explosion that occurs at the end of a large star's life.

Telescope (TEL-e-scope)   An instrument that gathers light from the sky and focuses it into an image. *See also* reflector telescope and refractor telescope.

Trillion (TRIL-yun)   A large number represented by a 1 followed by 12 zeros (1,000,000,000,000).

Twinkling (TWING-kling)   The bouncing around of a star's light caused by the moving air around us.

Universe (YOO-ni-vurss)   All the planets, stars, and galaxies that are known.

Zenith (ZEE-nith)   The place in the sky directly over your head.

Zodiac (ZO-dee-ak)   The band of stars and constellations through which the sun, moon, and planets appear to travel. The zodiac has 12 constellations.

Further Exploring

Once you know your way around the night sky, you may want to explore other books, magazines, and museums that will help you to learn more about what you've discovered in this book.

 Books

Album of Astronomy. Tom McGowen. New York: Checkerboard Press/Macmillan, 1987. 64 pages. $4.95.

Astronomy Today: Planets, Stars, Space Exploration. Dinah L. Moche, Ph.D. New York: Random House Library of Knowledge/Random House, 1982. 96 pages. $9.95.

Exploring the Night Sky: The Equinox Astronomy Guide for Beginners. Terence Dickinson. Ontario: Camden House Publishing, Ltd., 1987. 72 pages. $9.95.

The Friendly Stars. Martha Evans Martin and Donald Howard Menzel. New York: Dover Publications, Inc., 1964. 147 pages. $3.50.

The Nova Space Explorers Guide: Where to Go and What to See. Richard Maurer. New York: Clarkson N. Potter, Inc., 1985. 118 pages. $12.95.

Sky Challenger: Games for Star Gazers. Discovery Corner, Lawrence Hall of Science, Astronomy Education Program, Berkeley, CA. $6.95.

Stars. Herbert S. Zim and Robert H. Baker. New York: Golden Press/Western Publishing Co., 1985 (revised edition). $3.95.

Starlight Nights. Leslie C. Peltier. Cambridge, Massachusetts: Sky Publishing Corporation, 1980. 236 pages. $8.95.

Magazines

Abrams Planetarium Sky Calendar, published quarterly. $6.00 per year. Abrams Planetarium, Michigan State University, East Lansing, MI 48824. Set of monthly star charts including a daily guide for watching astronomical events.

Astronomy Magazine, published monthly. $21.00 per year; $30.00 outside the U.S. AstroMedia Corporation, 1027 North 7th Street, Milwaukee, WI 53233–1471. An advanced journal on current events in the world of astronomy.

Odyssey Magazine, published monthly. $19.95 per year; $23.95 outside the U.S. AstroMedia Corporation, 1027 North 7th Street, Milwaukee, WI 53233–1471. For young readers and beginning astronomers. Includes sky games and activities.

Sky and Telescope Magazine, published monthly. $21.95 per year, $25.45 outside the U.S. P.O. Box 9111 Belmont, MA 02178–9111. A hands-on journal for the actual sky observer. Articles about new equipment and ways of observing the night sky.

Maps

Your Own Star Map: The detail on the front jacket is taken from THE MAP OF THE UNIVERSE by Thomas Filsinger. It is available from the publisher in two versions: The Northern Hemisphere and The Southern Hemisphere. Both measure 36″×36″ and are printed in four-colors plus two varnishes. The non-toxic, phosphorescent ink GLOWS IN THE DARK. The price is $9.95 *each* plus $2.00 *each* for postage and handling. California residents *only* please add $.60 each for sales tax. Celestial Arts, P.O. Box 7327, Berkeley, CA 94707. (415) 524–1801

Planetariums, Observatories, and Space Museums

If you visit a planetarium, you'll be able to see examples of what the stars and planets look like and what times of the year they are best viewed. Planetariums give you a chance to see what the night sky would look like if you could see it without any light pollution. Some planetariums have special shows that highlight specific areas of the sky or astronomical events. It's a good idea to call ahead and find out what shows are playing and the starting times. The list below represents only a few of the planetariums, observatories, and space museums that you can visit. Check your telephone book or local library to find out if there are any in your area.

Arizona

Flandrau Planetarium. The University of Arizona, Corner of Cherry and University Boulevard, Tucson, AZ 85721. (602) 621–4515. Open Tuesday through Sunday.

California

Exploratorium. 3601 Lyon Street, San Francisco, CA 94123. (415) 563–7337. Open Wednesday through Sunday.

Griffith Observatory. 2800 East Observatory Road, Los Angeles, CA 90027. (213) 664–1191. Open Tuesday through Sunday; open Mondays in the summer.

Lawrence Hall of Science. The University of California at Berkeley, Berkeley, CA 94720. (415) 642–5134. Open Monday through Sunday.

Morrison Planetarium. California Academy of Sciences, Golden Gate Park, San Francisco, CA 94118. (415) 750–7141. Open Monday through Sunday.

Reuben H. Fleet Space Theater and Science Center. 1875 El Prado, Balboa Park, San Diego, CA 92101. (619) 238–1233. Open Monday through Sunday.

Colorado

Fiske Planetarium and Science Center. University of Colorado, Boulder, CO 80309–0408. (303) 492–5001. Open Monday through Friday.

The Gates Planetarium. City Park, Denver, CO 80205. (303) 370–6351. Open Monday through Sunday.

District of Columbia

Albert Einstein Planetarium. National Air and Space Museum, Smithsonian Institution, 6th and Independence Avenue, S.W., Washington, D.C. 20560. (202) 357–1529. Open Monday through Sunday.

Florida

Astronaut Memorial Hall. 1519 Clearlake Road, Cocoa, FL 32926. (407) 632–1111. Open Monday through Saturday.

Bishop Planetarium. 201 10th Street West, Bradenton, FL 34205. (813) 746–4132. Open Tuesday through Sunday.

Alexander Brest Planetarium. Jacksonville Museum of Science and History, 1025 Gulf Life Drive, Jacksonville, FL 32207. (904) 396–7062. Open Monday through Sunday.

NASA Kennedy Space Center's Spaceport USA. TWRS Kennedy Space Center, FL 32899. (407) 452–2121. Open Monday through Sunday.

Miami Space Transit Planetarium. 3280 South Miami Avenue, Miami, FL 33129. (305) 854–2222. Open Monday through Sunday.

Georgia

Fernbank Science Center. 156 Heaton Park Drive NE, Atlanta, GA 30307. (404) 378–4311. Open Monday through Sunday.

Hawaii

Bishop Museum Planetarium. 1525 Bernice Street, Honolulu, HI 96817. (808) 847–3511. Open Monday through Saturday and the first Sunday of every month.

Illinois

Adler Planetarium. 1300 South Lake Shore Drive, Chicago, IL 60605. (312) 322–0337. Open Monday through Sunday.

Museum of Science and Industry and Crown Space Center. 57th Street and Lake Shore Drive, Chicago, IL 60636. (312) 684–1414. Open Monday through Sunday.

Kansas

Kansas Cosmosphere and Space Center. 1100 North Plum, Hutchinson, KS 67501. (316) 662–2305. Open Monday through Sunday.

Wichita Omnisphere and Science Center. 220 South Main Street, Wichita, KS 67202. (316) 264–3174. Open Tuesday through Sunday.

Maryland

Maryland Science Center. 601 Light Street, Baltimore, MD 21230. (301) 685–5225. Open Monday through Sunday.

Massachusetts

Harvard/Smithsonian Center for Astrophysics. 60 Garden Street, Cambridge, MA 02138. (617) 495–7461. Open third Thursday evening of every month.

Charles Hayden Planetarium—Boston Museum of Science. Science Park, Boston, MA 02114–1099. (617) 589–0270. Open Monday through Sunday.

Michigan

Abrams Planetarium. Michigan State University, East Lansing, MI 48824. (517) 355–4676. Public shows Saturday and Sunday.

Robert B. Chaffee Planetarium. Grand Rapids Public Museum, 233 Washington SE, Grand Rapids, MI 49503. (616) 456–3985. Open Monday through Sunday.

Mississippi

Ronald E. McNair Space Theater/Russell Davis Planetarium. 201 East Pascagoula Street, Jackson, MS 39201. (601) 960–1550. Open Tuesday through Sunday.

Missouri

St. Louis Science Center. 5050 Oakland Avenue, St. Louis, MO 63110. (314) 289–4444. Open Monday through Sunday.

Nevada

Fleischmann Planetarium. University of Nevada–Reno, Reno, NV 89557. (702) 784–4812. Open Monday through Sunday.

New Mexico

The Space Center. Top of New Mexico Highway 2001, Box 533, Alamogordo, NM 88310. (505) 437–2840. Open Monday through Sunday.

New York

American Museum/Hayden Planetarium. Central Park West at 81st Street, New York, NY 10024–5192. (212) 769–5900. Open Monday through Sunday.

Strasenburgh Planetarium. Rochester Museum and Science Center, 657 East Avenue, Rochester, NY 14607. (716) 271–4320. Open Monday through Sunday.

Vanderbilt Museum and Planetarium. 178 Little Neck Road, Centerport, NY 11721. (516) 262–7800. Open Tuesday through Sunday.

North Carolina

Discovery Place and Nature Museum. 301 North

Tryon Street, Charlotte, NC 28202. (704) 332–4140. Open Monday through Sunday.

Ohio

Visitor Center at NASA's Lewis Research Center. 21000 Brookpark Road, Cleveland, OH 44135. (216) 433–2004. Open Monday through Sunday.

Oregon

Oregon Museum of Science and Industry/Harry C. Kendall Planetarium. 4015 SW Canyon Road, Portland, OR 97221. (503) 222–2828. Open Monday through Sunday.

Pennsylvania

Buhl Science Center. Allegheny Square, Pittsburgh, PA 15212. (412) 237–3300. Open Monday through Sunday.

Franklin Institute/Fels Planetarium. 20th and the Parkway, Philadelphia, PA 19103. (215) 448–1293, or (215) 448–1200. Open Monday through Sunday.

Tennessee

Memphis Pink Palace Museum and Planetarium. 3050 Central Avenue, Memphis, TN 38111. (901) 454–5609. Open Tuesday through Sunday.

Texas

Lyndon B. Johnson Space Center/Olin Teague Visitor Center. 2101 NASA Road 1, Public Services Branch, AP4, Houston, TX 77058. (713) 483–4241. Open Monday through Sunday.

McDonald Observatory/W.L. Moody Visitor's Center. P.O. Box 1337, Fort Davis, TX 79734. (915) 426–3263. Open Monday through Sunday.

Utah

Hansen Planetarium. 15 South State Street, Salt Lake City, UT 84111. (801) 538–2104. Open Monday through Sunday.

Virginia

NASA Langley Visitor Center. Mail Stop 480, Hampton, VA 23665. (804) 864–6000. Open Monday through Sunday.

Science Museum of Virginia/Universe Space Theater. 2500 West Broad Street, Richmond, VA 23220. (804) 367–1013. Open Tuesday through Sunday. Open Mondays in the summer.

Wallops Flight Facility's NASA Visitor Center. Wallops Island, VA 23337. (804) 824–2298. Open Thursday through Monday. Open seven days a week in the summer.

Washington

Pacific Science Center. 200 Second Avenue North, Seattle, WA 98109. (206) 443–2001. Open Monday through Sunday.

West Virginia

National Radio Astronomy Observatory. P.O. Box 2, Green Bank, WV 24944–0002. (304) 456–2011. Open Monday through Sunday, mid-June through Labor Day.

Canada

B.C. Space Sciences Center/H.R. McMillan Planetarium. 1100 Chestnut Street, Vancouver BJ6 3J9. (604) 736–4331.. Open Monday through Sunday.

Dow Planetarium. 1000, rue de St. Jacques West, Montreal, Quebec H3C 1G7. (514) 872–4530. Open Monday through Sunday.

Edmonton Space Sciences Centre. 11211–142 Street, Edmonton, Alberta T5M 4A1. (403) 452–9100. Open Tuesday through Sunday.

McLaughlin Planetarium. 100 Queen's Park, Toronto, Ontario M5S 2C6. (416) 586–5736. Open Tuesday through Sunday.

Ontario Science Centre. 770 Don Mills Road, Toronto, Ontario M3C 1T3. (416) 429–0193. Open Monday through Sunday.

Index

See also Glossary, pages 81–83.

Page numbers in *italics* refer to illustrations.

Ahnighito (meteorite), *56*
Al Anz, distance to, 66
Aldebaran, 29
Alphirk, distance to, 66
Altair, distance to, 66
altitude, 67
amateur astronomers, 79–80
American Indians, 31, 57
American Museum of Natural
    History, Hayden Planetarium,
    56, 57
American satellites, 14
ancient stargazers, 8, 51, 56
Andromeda Galaxy, 31, 65, 66, 74
annular eclipses, 52, 54
Antarctica, 58
Antares, 28
Aquarius (water-bearer), 36
Aquila (eagle), 32
Arabic language, 10
archer (Sagittarius), 36
Arcturus, distance to, 66
Arecibo, Puerto Rico, *78*
Aries (ram), 32, 36
Arizona, 57
asterisms, 32–33

astrology, 35
astronauts, *45*
astronomers, 75–80, *79*
astronomy vs. astrology, 35
Atlas, 31
aurora borealis, *22*
autumn, sky map for, *27*
averted vision, 10
azimuth, 68

Bay of Rainbows, 43
bear (Ursa Major), 31, *31,* 32
Bennett Comet, 58
Betelgeuse, 11
Big Dipper, *22,* 23, 29, 31, 32, 40
    brightest star in, 65
Blackfoot Indians, 31
blue stars, 10
bolides, 57
Boötes (herdsman), 33
bull (Taurus), 36

Callisto (Jupiter moon), 73, *73*
Cancer (crab), 36
Canis Minor (dog), 32
Cape Florida, *59*
Cape York Meteorite "Ahnighito,"
    56
Capricornus (she-goat), 36
Cassiopeia, 32
Cepheus, 31–32
Cetus, 32, 36
circumpolar stars, 40
"Cl," 21
Clouds, Sea of (moon), 44
cluster of stars, 21

colors
    changing, in sky, 13
    of daytime sky, 12–13
    of stars, 10
comets, 58, *58*
constellations, 21, 31, 32
corona, of sun, *51,* 52
cosmic dust, 56
crab (Cancer), 36
craters, on moon, 48, *49*
crescent moon, 45
Cygnus (swan), 11

dark-adapted vision, 9
degrees, 67
Deneb (tail), 11, 66
Dipper
    Big, *22,* 23, 29, 31, 32, 40, 65
    Little, *56*
direct motion, 17
directions, describing, 21
distances, 62–68
    cosmic, 66
    in light years, *64*
dog (Canis Minor), 32
dragons, 31
Dreams, Lake of (moon), 43, 44
Dubhe, 65, 66
dust, cosmic, 56

eagle (Aquila), 32
Earth, 16, *18*
    distance of moon from, 64
    revolution of, 40, *40*
    rotation of, 38–40, *40*
    shadow of, 13

speed of, 40
  star closest to, 64
eastern sky, at sunset, 13
eclipses, 50–54, *51*
  annular, 52, 54
  danger of viewing, 52
  of moon, 53, *53,* 54
  total, *51*
  upcoming, 54
Europa (Jupiter moon), 73, *73*
exploding star, *65*
eyepieces, 70

fall, sky map for, *27*
falling stars, 55–61
fireballs, 57
first-quarter moon, 45, *47*
fish (Pisces), 36
flashlight, 9, *10*
Foam, Sea of (moon), 44
France, 52, 57
full moon, 46, *47*

galaxies, *8, 17,* 21, 64, 74
  Andromeda, 31, 65, 66, 74
  Milky Way, 8, *17,* 74
  spiral, *63*
Galilean satellites, *73*
Ganymede (Jupiter moon), 73, *73*
Gemini (twins), 36
Germany, 52
gibbous phase of moon, 45
"Glx," 21
gods, 31
  eclipse as warning from, 51
  planets as, 35

gravity, of moon, *43*
Great Andromeda Galaxy, 31, 65,
  66, 74
Great Orion Nebula, 74
Great Square of Pegasus, 33, 65
Great Winter Circle, 33
Greek legends, 31

Halley's Comet, 58
Hayden Planetarium, *56,* 57
Hercules, 31
  star cluster in, 74
herdsman (Boötes), 33
heroes, 31
Hi and Ho, 51
horizon, 21
horoscope, 35
hunter (Orion), 11, 23, 29, 41
hurricanes, satellite photographs of,
  76

Io (Jupiter moon), 73, *73*
Italy, 52

Jupiter, 16, 17, 18, *73*
  through telescope, 73
  moons of, 73

kite, 33
Kitt Peak National Observatory, 76

Lacus Somniorum (moon), 44
Lake of Dreams (moon), 43, 44
last quarter moon, *47*
lava, on moon, 43
lens, in telescope, 70

Leo (lion), 23, 28, 33, 36
Libra (scales), 36
light, speed of, 64
light buckets, 70
light pollution, 8
light years, 65
  distances in, *64*
lion (Leo), 23, 28, 33, 36
Little Dipper, *56*
logbook, 8–9, *9*
Louis, Emperor of Bavaria, 52
lunar eclipses, *51,* 53, *53,* 54

magnet, for collecting
  micrometeorites, 61
maiden (Virgo), 36
maria (seas), on moon, 44
Mars, 16, 17, 18, *18,* 58
Marsh of Mists (moon), 44
Mercury, 16, 17
Meteor Crater (Arizona), *57*
meteor showers, 59, *59,* 60
meteorites, 57
  Cape York Meteorite "Ahnighito,"
  56
  on moon, *49*
meteoroids, 56
meteors, 55–61, *56*
micrometeorites, 61
Milky Way Galaxy, 8, *17,* 74
  twin galaxy of, 65
MIR Space Station, Soviet, 14
mirror, in telescope, 70
Mists, Marsh of (moon), 44
moon, 42–49
  astronauts on, *45*

Bay of Rainbows on, 43
craters on, 48, *49*
crescent, 45
distance from Earth, 64
eclipse of, 53
first-quarter, *47*
full, 46, *47*
gibbous phase of, 45
gravity of, *43*
Lake of Dreams on, 43, 44
lava on, 43
Marsh of Mists on, 44
meteorites on, *49*
mountains on, 44
new, 46, *46*
phases of, 43
seas on, 43, 44
shape of, 43, 45–46
through telescope, 72, *72*
moons, of Jupiter, 73
motion, 37
  direct, 17
  retrograde, 18
mountains, on moon, 44
movement, of stars, 39

names, of stars, 10–11, 21
"Nb," 21
nebula, 21, *65*, 74
Nectar, Sea of (moon), 44
Neptune, 16
new moon, 46, *46*
night vision, 9–10
North Pole, 38
North Star (Polaris), 29, 40

observatories, 79, 85–87
Ocean of Storms (moon), 43, 44
ocean tides, moon gravity and, *43*
Oceanus Procellarum (moon), 44
Ophiuchus, 36
opposition, 18
orange stars, 10
Orion (hunter), 11, 23, 29, 41
Orion Nebula, 74

Palus Nebularum (moon), 44
partial lunar eclipse, *53*
partial solar eclipse, 52
Pegasus, Great Square of, 33, 65
Perseus, 32
  meteor shower in, 59
phases, of moon, 43
Pisces (fish), 36
planetariums, 85–87
planets
  as gods, 35
  movement of, 17
  position of in sky, 16
  through telescope, 72
  vs. stars, 15–18
Pleiades, 31, 74
  distance to, 66
Pluto, 16
pointer stars, 29
Polaris (North Star), 29, 40
  distance to, 66
pollution, light, 8
Polynesians, 31
position, measurement of, 68
Proxima Centauri, 64
purple, in eastern sky at sunset, 13

radio telescope, 78
Rainbows, Bay of (moon), 43
ram (Aries), 32, 36
red light, 9, *10*
reflector telescopes, 69, *70*
refractor telescopes, 69, *70*
Regulus, 28, 66
retrograde motion, 18
revolution of Earth, 40, *40*
rotation of Earth, 38–40, *40*

Sagittarius (archer), 36
satellites, 13–14
  Galilean, *73*
  hurricane photograph from, 76
  Skylab space station, *14*
  speed of, 68
  Tiros, *13*
Saturn, 16, 17, *17*, 18
  through telescope, 73
scales (Libra), 36
Scorpius (scorpion), 23, 36, 41
seas, on moon, 43, 44
Serenity, Sea of (moon), 44
Seven Beauties, 31–32
shadow of Earth, 13
she-goat (Capricornus), 36
shooting stars, 8, 55–61
showers, of meteors, 59, *59*, 60
signs, astrological, 35
Sirius, 29, 65, 66
sky
  changes in, from revolution, 41
  color of in daytime, 12–13
  dividing, 32
  eastern, at sunset, 13

measuring, 67
monthly changes in, 23
sky maps, 20–23, *24–27*, 28
Skylab space station, *14*
solar eclipses
    danger of viewing, 52
    total, *51*
    upcoming, 54
South Pole, 38
Southern Sea (moon), 44
Soviet satellites, 14
space museums, 85–87
Space Shuttle (U.S.), 14, 77
speed
    of Earth, 40
    of light, 64
Spica, distance to, 66
spiral galaxies, *63*
sporadic meteors, 57
spring, sky map for, *25*
Square of Pegasus, 65
star clusters, 74
star map, 19. *See also* sky maps
stargazers, 8–10
starhopping, 29
stars
    circumpolar, 40
    closest to Earth, 64
    clusters of, 21
    colors of, 10
    discovering, 10–11
    exploding, *65*
    groupings of, 21
    movement of, 39
    names of, 10–11, 21
    shooting, 8

stories of, 30–36
through telescope, 73–74
twinkling of, 10, 16
vs. planets, 15–18
stories, of stars, 30–36
Storms, Ocean of (moon), 43, 44
summer sky, 41
    map for, *26*
Summer Triangle, 33
sun
    corona of, *51*
    danger of looking at, 71
    Earth's distance from, 64
    viewing safely, *71*
sun filter, 71
sun projector, 52, *52*
sunlight, time to reach Earth, 64
suns, stars as, 10
sunset, 13
sunspots, 71–72
supernova, *65*
swan (Cygnus), 11

tail (Deneb), 11
tail, of comet, 58
Taurus (bull), 33, 36
telescopes, 69–74, 79
    building, 74
    examining sun with, 71
    moon through, 72, *72*
    parts of, 70
    planets through, 73
    radio, *78*
    reflector, 69, *70*
    refractor, 69, *70*
    stars through, 73–74

Tiros satellite, *13*
total lunar eclipse, *51*, 53
total solar eclipse, 51, *51*
Tranquility, Sea of (moon), 43, 44
Trapezium, 73
tripod, 70
tube, of telescope, 70
twinkling, 10, 16
twins (Gemini), 36

United States Skylab space station,
    14
Uranus, 16
Ursa Major, 31, *31*, 32

Vapors, Sea of (moon), 44
Vega, 10
Venus, 16, 17
    through telescope, 73
Virgo (maiden), 36
vision
    averted, 9
    dark-adapted, 9
    night, 9–10
Voyager spacecraft, *73*

Wan Ho, 42–43
water-bearer (Aquarius), 36
Winter Circle, Great, 33
winter sky, 41
    map for, *24*

zenith, 21
zodiac, 35–36
Zubenelgenubi, 10

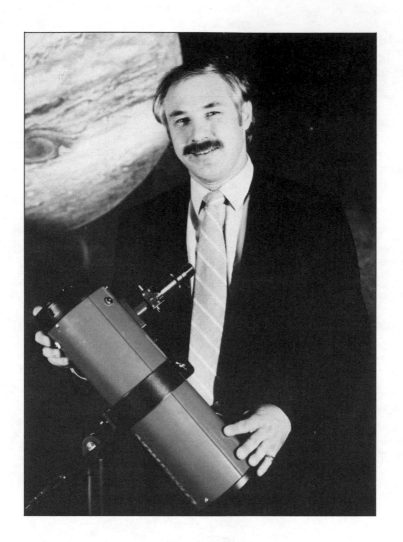

About the Author

Dennis Mammana is Resident Astronomer and Director of Production for the Reuben H. Fleet Space Theater and Science Center at Balboa Park in San Diego. He has written for *Odyssey* magazine and other science publications. He has been stargazing since he was seven years old.